RIDE HARD RIDE SMART

Ultimate Street Strategies for Advanced Motorcyclists

Pat Hahn

MOTORBOOKS
INTERNATIONAL

To my wife, Kristin, and my family. They are the reasons I work so hard at staying safe.

Library of Congress Cataloging-in-Publication Data
Hahn, Pat, 1969-
Ride hard, ride smart / by Pat Hahn
      p. cm.
ISBN 0-7603-1760-7 (pbk.)
   1. Motorcycling--Safety measures. 2. Traffic safety.
   3. Motorcycling accidents--Prevention. I. Title.

TL440.5H36 2004
629.28'475'0289--dc22

On the front cover: Kawasaki's awesome 2004 Z1000. Copyright Kawasaki, photo used with permission

On the frontispiece: We live in this world. We know absolutely nothing about 99.9 percent of the people in it. We're surely all very, very different, and yet there is an undeniable fact: We have to share the same roadways.

On the title page: An example of shadowing: Keep mental notes on the intersections in which you can use another vehicle to run interference for you. Keeping a large vehicle nearby as you ride, or riding from large vehicle to large vehicle, works too.

On the back cover: Knowing your surroundings, in front of you, behind you, and from side to side, is one of the fundamental keys to survival on the road.

Edited by Darwin Holmstrom
Designed by Stephanie Michaud

Printed in Hong Kong

ACKNOWLEDGMENTS

Dirk Koenig coauthored Chapter 2, "Getting Hurt 101."

Thanks to the Minnesota Sportbike group (www.MN-Sportbike.org), my muse. You have taught me how to ride and how to have fun doing it. I couldn't wish for a more enthusiastic and generous group of friends. You people rock.

Thanks to Andy Goldfine and the gang at the Rider WearHouse. Your products make motorcycling better. Time is something that cannot be bought or created, but a Roadcrafter suit makes more of it available for riding.

Thanks to Darwin Holmstrom, Kim Halvorson, Dale Borgeson, Vic Wanchena, John Gateley, and Jeff Giacomini—without Jeff, neither Veemax Vince nor this book would exist.

Thanks to Darrin Behrens; Dave Bergan; Joe Birchhill; Jason Bishop; John Borchert; Corey Canfield; Gig Cimmino; Tom Day; Rafael Demay; Timmy Erickson and Victory Motorcycles; John Griffith, Quinn, Sean, and Annie McGrath; Uncle Pat Hahn; Deron Harris; Brent Jass; Jonah Klevesahl; Kent Larson; Tony Marx; Kyle and Carrie Ohnstad; Julien and Lou Olson; George O'Neill; Michael Pilhofer; Greg Polanski; Jeff Sanders; Dennis Sullivan; Tony Kellen; Robert Ogden; Robin Ogle; Karl Rehpohl; Teri Seaman; and Blake Stranz.

CONTENTS

If you learn one thing from this book, learn to take motorcycling seriously. That more than anything else is what will save your life.

If you were going to go skydiving, you wouldn't just hop on the plane, throw a pack over your shoulder, and jump, would you? You'd learn how to skydive. You'd take the training. You'd learn when to jump, how to jump, how your chute works, how to use it, and how to land.

Would you go rock climbing without preparing yourself? Would you just grab some rope and try to scale a mountain? Would you do it after a couple of beers? Would you just go in your shoes and T-shirt and climb like you climb stairs? No,

If you were going to go skydiving, you wouldn't just hop on the plane, throw a pack over your shoulder, and jump, would you? You'd learn how to skydive.

At first, tying your shoe is a lot of work and requires 100 percent of your attention. But eventually, your hands learn to do the trick and you can free your mind up for other things.

The three degrees of separation: defensive riding strategy, training and skills, and riding gear.

you wouldn't. You'd learn how to do it. You'd use good gear. You'd take precautions to ensure your safety in a risky activity. It only hurts if you fall.

Would you go scuba diving without preparing yourself for it? Would you dive without knowing how much air you had in your tank? You wouldn't. You'd prepare. You'd have all the right equipment and you'd do it right. You'd take the necessary precautions, you'd stay within your limits, and you'd follow the rules. Anything else would be suicide.

Motorcycling is just like that. It's not dangerous until you screw up. If you do screw up, it very well could mean your life. So you take precautions. You know your limits. You prepare your mind and your body. You know your equipment. And you know what you're getting yourself into. You're aware of the risks, and you're consciously managing them. An intelligent motorcyclist does everything in his or her power to reduce the risks.

Three simple rules can help you minimize the risks you take on your motorcycle:

Rule 1: Predict the future and assure your place in it.

Rule 2: The more you practice, the luckier you get.

Rule 3: You can prevent every crash.

The Three Degrees of Separation

This book is for the risk-averse rider in all of us.

I'm going to assume quite a bit. I'm going to assume that you already know how to operate a motorcycle. I'm going to

assume that you have a few years of riding under your belt. I'm going to assume you've already taken the three critical steps you can take to increase your safety: you use a riding strategy to predict and avoid hazards, you've taken rider skills training, and you wear protective gear.

I call these steps the "three degrees of separation." These three factors, in that order, are all that stands between you and almost certain death.

Think of the three degrees of separation as a pyramid, with riding strategy as the base, rider training in the middle, and protective gear at the top. They overlap to form the basic structure of safe motorcycling.

The first chapter presents the basic principles of the three degrees of separation, and will be a springboard into the subtler aspects of motorcycle safety. If what I give you here regarding riding strategy, training, and protective gear isn't enough, there is plenty of good reading out there to help, like *The Complete Idiot's Guide to Motorcycling*, *The Motorcycle Safety Foundation's Guide to Motorcycling Excellence*, *Proficient Motorcycling*, *Total Control*, and the Web sites motorcyclesafety.state.mn.us and msgroup.org.

To successfully use the rest of this book, you, the reader, will need to commit to a few basic requirements necessary to practice the three degrees of separation. I want you to have taken the training, and I want you to practice your skills. I want you to wear all the necessary gear—the best gear out there. Get the best suit, the best helmet, the best boots, and the best gloves. Treat yourself—you'll be glad you did. Even

Get the best suit, the best helmet, the best boots, and the best gloves. Treat yourself—you'll be glad you did.

On a motorcycle, your life depends on your ability to do two things at once.

beyond the protection the best gear offers in a crash, high-quality gear makes riding safely easier, because it increases your physical comfort. This book is full of examples of what I consider the best gear in the world for a street rider.

The strategies presented in the remaining chapters are intended to supplement the three degrees. The fundamentals of the three degrees are critical to your survival; the twists and oddments presented in these pages should be piled on top of those fundamentals.

Learning to ride a motorcycle is like learning to tie your shoes. The first few times are bewildering. Someone coaches you from point A to point B, but you don't remember how you got there. You have to talk yourself through it—over, under, in and out—and it's frustrating and time consuming. You make mistakes. You tie really horrible knots. But you learn. You get better, and before too long you can tie your shoes quickly and with nice, square knots. You don't need to think about it anymore. Tying your shoes becomes something of a nonissue, something you can do while watching TV or talking on the phone. You have that extra bit of mental time to spare because your body is taking care of the details.

On a motorcycle, your life depends on your ability to do two things at once.

Myth has it that humans only use about 10 percent of their brains. Motorcyclists who actively use the three degrees are probably only using about 10 percent of their motorcycling brains. But once you've got those three degrees down, locked in, once they're second nature, and you do them without even thinking about it, like tying your shoes, you're ready to kick it up a notch and get more out of your motorcycle brain. With the help of this book, maybe you can use 11 percent of your motorcycling brain.

I don't claim to be anything other than ordinary. I am a completely average, avid motorcyclist. What I lack in riding skills and hazard awareness I try to make up for with the concepts in this book. I am aware of my weaknesses and work to keep them in the background by not putting myself into bad situations in the first place. I'm a defensive-minded, analytical motorcycle enthusiast who is deathly afraid of pain. I internalized the three degrees to minimize my exposure to pain, then set out to learn more.

And there is more—that's what this book's about—but if you're already using the three degrees, you can only plug leaks and make small fortifications to your (already formidable) defenses. To take your risk avoidance to the next level, you need to

The fact that you are interested in motorcycle safety means that your biggest risk is probably not yourself; it's your environment.

work on hazard mitigation by preparing your mind, body, and bike so well that you avoid the hazardous circumstances in the first place.

I'm an average rider who is extremely concerned with my own safety. When riding a motorcycle I do everything I can to prolong my life. Call it my motorcycle conscience: I owe it to myself and my family to exert as much control as possible over every element of risk.

The fact that you are interested in motorcycle safety means that your biggest risk is probably not yourself; it's your environment. Thus it is important to analyze

what the other guy is doing, which will be a major focus in the following chapters. I want to give you some new ways of looking at the art of self-preservation.

Hundreds of factors contribute to a motorcycle crash. You make hundreds of decisions, some conscious, some not, on your motorcycle every day. Some decisions involve crashing, some involve avoiding a crash, and some don't involve crashes at all. Making a decision without a reason, making a decision without choosing— that's gambling. Don't leave your fate up to chance. Control what you can. Make your choices for *a reason*.

USING THE THREE DEGREES OF SEPARATION

On your motorcycle, four things separate you from the ground: a riding strategy that requires aggressive attention and sound decision making, rider training, superior physical skills, and your protective riding gear, in that order. After that, it's just you and the pavement. Each of these things, by itself, can protect you. Combined, they create a strong defense against the potential hazards involved with motorcycling.

Riding Strategy–Predicting the Future and Assuring Your Place in It

Mental skills make up 90 percent of everyday riding. This is your first degree of separation. Once you've mastered the mechanical controls and become used to your bike, normal operation becomes almost automatic. As you gain more and more riding experience, you become comfortable and confident. But this doesn't make you a better rider. It only frees up your brain from the distraction of the controls. *This* allows you to develop your first line of defense: a riding strategy. One hundred percent attention to your surroundings, accurate detection and perception of road hazards and risks, and sound judgment and decision

An example of the vanashing point. Standing between the rails, see how they seem to come together way off in the distance? Pat Hahn

If you haven't done so, studying and applying the various approaches to riding strategy is an absolute must. Start with *The Motorcycle Safety Foundation's Guide to Riding Excellence*, follow it up with David Hough's books *Proficient Motorcycling*, throw in the *Police Rider's Handbook*, and top it all off with Lee Parks' *Total Control*. These four books should give you a good base from which to start developing a master strategy.

Riding Strategies

Riding a motorcycle into traffic without a game plan is ignorant at best, suicide at worst. A continuous mental process of absorbing information, analyzing it, and preemptively using it to avoid mistakes is crucial to a rider's survival. There are several formal driving strategies. Each is an organized system to process information, each attempts to identify and avoid hazards, and each is fairly simple to use. Most skilled riders have invented or adapted one or more of them to their own riding style and their own needs.

If you don't yet have a riding strategy, the best place to begin is in a Motorcycle Safety Foundation basic or experienced rider course. Each course includes a substantial mental component along with practice using that component. Both courses use the Search, Evaluate, and Execute (SEE) sequence as a tool for dealing with any sort of hazard. Both place heaviest emphasis on the "evaluate" stage of the process: playing the "What if?" game, in which riders imagine and prepare for any number of possible scenarios that might put them at risk. Both also work hard to ensure clear mind and body communication, accurate information collection and perception, and swift and purposeful reactions to possible hazards.

Other formal strategies exist, as well. The best I've seen was explained in *Motorcycle Roadcraft*, a handbook for police riders in Europe. This is a very physical strategy that takes the whole of Scan, Identify, Predict, Decide and Execute (SIPDE) and Scan, Plan, Act (SPA) and combines them into one step: Information. From there, the rider then makes adjustments based on the most important physical aspects of his or her relationship to the hazard: Position, Speed, Gear, and Acceleration, in that order. It's not that this strategy downplays the information/SEE stage, but rather assumes you already use it, just as I assume it in this book.

While this book assumes you already use riding strategies based on formal training, research, and experience, I believe a few strategies could be addressed in more detail in many of the available resources. I don't mean to imply that these are the particular mental constructs you must use if you are to have a riding strategy. These are merely good places to begin. Every rider eventually develops his or her own. It's just important to have a good place to start, and to know one or two that work for other people.

Cornering Strategies

With the exception of the book *Total Control*, I don't think enough is written or said about where the rider should look in a corner.

At the most basic level, successful cornering relies heavily on your perception of the radius of a curve. Think of this as trying to understand what the road is doing. We'll ignore for the moment the roles that road crown, motorcycle design, tires, and rider inputs play, and concentrate only on the curve itself.

Cornering speed derives directly from the radius of the curve. The sharper the curve or the smaller the radius, the slower a rider needs to travel to stay safely within his or her limits.

Conversely, the wider a curve or the larger a radius, the faster a rider can go and still be within reasonable safety margins.

Riding a motorcycle into traffic without a game plan is ignorant at best, suicide at worst.

The radius also determines the turn-in point, or the point at which the rider spots the exit and throws the bike in and commits to the turn, heading for the apex. An increasing-radius turn allows the rider to toss the bike in early. A constant radius should be apexed at the center of the turn. A decreasing radius relies on the rider throwing the bike in late and apexing late. This is a basic principle of high-performance riding, but it is also an important aspect of safe riding.

The radius also tells the rider when to begin accelerating again. Once the turn begins to widen, that's the rider's cue to roll on the throttle. If a turn tightens up again, it's time to decrease speed.

The problems are that no two curves are alike and road signs don't tell us much about the radius of a curve. The most we get is a recommended speed—and even those advisories are not consistent from state to state and even county to county. So how does a rider get a feel for the radius of a turn without getting off the bike at every bend with a compass, measuring tape, chalk, pen, and notebook?

The key is in the vanishing point—the same one used in Art 101 classes to teach students to draw in perspective. Simply put, the vanishing point (referred to in *Motorcycle Roadcraft* as a "limit point") is the exact point where the two sides of the road appear to come together somewhere on the horizon. This imaginary point can help you determine your speed, your turn-in, and your roll-on. In addition to all that, it gives you the direction and approximate distance upon which you should point your head and eyes for directional control of the motorcycle.

The cardinal rule of cornering is that you set your speed so that you are able to execute an emergency stop within the amount of road that you can see. You want to be riding slowly enough so that you are able to stop before you reach the vanishing point. While riding through a corner, the vanishing point is the point where the left and right sides of the road converge or, in some cases, the place where the road disappears behind a hill, trees, or some other visual obstruction.

If you're in too hot and overcommit yourself, any surprises will likely cause a crash. You also want to set your entry speed before the turn-in point. At the turn-in point you want to be done slowing and ready to accelerate out of the turn. As you approach and ride through a bend, the position of the vanishing point will move relative to you. Sometimes it will move toward you, sometimes away, and sometimes it will seem to be stationary. What it's doing at any given moment should tell you what to be doing at the same moment.

Focusing on the vanishing point will help you judge the proper entrance speed into a corner. Remember that the radius of the curve determines the proper speed for the corner. Radius and speed change as your position within the turn changes. The vanishing point is the most consistent indicator of the radius of a corner, and the easiest to read. Observing the "behavior" of the vanishing point can help you determine exactly what the bend is doing.

The goal of this technique is that you adjust your speed with respect to how the visual point appears to be moving. If the visual point moves toward you, you decelerate. If it moves away from you, you accelerate.

As you approach a turn, the visual point will start moving toward you. The faster it moves toward you, generally, the tighter the bend. As you close in on the visual point you should be decelerating or at least maintaining a constant speed and keeping to the outside of the turn. The faster the visual point moves toward you the more pronounced your deceleration should be. Remember that you should still be able to stop within the roadway that you can see.

In many instances, for a short period of time, the vanishing point will stop moving. As you sweep through the corner, the imaginary focus point will seem to remain a constant distance from you. At this point you are in a constant-radius portion of the turn. Depending on the curve's geometry, this condition may continue for some time or only last an instant, and then the visual point will start to recede. In any case, the moment in which you stop closing in on the visual is your turn-in point for the bend, and the point at which your are no longer slowing. At this point, you should roll on the throttle slightly in anticipation

Your reference point is very close to you. Your speed should reflect the distance between you and that point. In an emergency, you may need to be able to stop the bike before you get there.

of the exit. This slight acceleration settles the motorcycle's suspension and makes it more stable.

When the vanishing point moves away from you, it indicates that the curve is widening. This is the point at which you begin the drive out of the turn. You are now chasing the visual point. The faster it moves away from you the more you can stand the bike up and the harder you can accelerate. As the curve widens, the vanishing point will very rapidly seem to disappear. The two sides of the road in your immediate path of travel will separate. This usually indicates the end of the bend.

Be careful here and don't get too carried away. Just because the vanishing point is moving away is no guarantee that you can stop in the distance available. You still have to know your limits. Also, the turn could tighten up again, and you don't want to be wringing the bike's neck when this happens. Until you can clearly see that the vanishing point completely disappears, you are still at some risk of corner-related problems.

In addition to the reference point defined by the roadway, there are other indicators that you can use to predict what a turn may do. Fences, tree lines, and utility poles often indicate where the roadway is going and will often give you a hint before the vanishing point indicates the same thing. Fences and utility poles usually follow property lines or rights of way. Beware, though, that these imaginary lines often follow a constant distance from the roadway, but sometimes they disappear into the trees. And sometimes they lie. The road may curve one way, but the tree line or utility poles might follow a driveway or fence line.

A word of caution: Don't try to learn this on your bike! Until finding and following the vanishing point becomes second nature, it takes a lot more mental energy than most motorcyclists have to spare. Start slow. Practice using the vanishing point while riding shotgun in someone else's car. With no other distractions, you'll learn to spot it easily and to recognize quickly whether it's coming or going. Spend as much time as necessary practicing this until you become proficient at reading a road, and then graduate to practicing in your own car while driving. You should not try it on your motorcycle until you're able to track the vanishing point using your peripheral vision and subconscious mind. That way you can devote most of your brain to spotting hazards.

Taking Responsibility for the Other Guy

Taking responsibility for your own actions is easy, but you, the motorcyclist, will more likely suffer bodily harm in the event of a crash. Therefore you, the motorcyclist, must take responsibility for everyone else's actions as well. This means being tuned into not only yourself, your bike, and your environment, but also being aware of other drivers, correctly anticipating their behavior, and effectively avoiding hazards before they place you at risk. Ideally, a skilled rider avoids hazards before they even *become* hazards. This level of ability doesn't come easily or naturally. It needs to be learned and aggressively practiced. An MSF rider training course can be a great place to start working on your attitude. Not only do you prepare yourself for riding, but you also get to explore your limits, and those limits include the

Taking responsibility for your own actions is easy, but you, the motorcyclist, will more likely suffer bodily harm in the event of a crash. Therefore you, the motorcyclist, must take responsibility for everyone else's actions as well.

On a motorcycle, his problem automatically becomes your problem if you want to stay safe.

Since the 1970s, the Motorcycle Safety Foundation (MSF) has focused on training riders in the fine art of riding safely. No rider should be on the street without a certain understanding of the fundamentals taught by the MSF. One call to (800) 446-9227 will point you to the course nearest you.

concepts of rider responsibility and risk management.

Attitude

Attitude plays an important part in riding strategy. Your attitude will determine how you will react in any given situation. Because your brain is your first and best defense, being aware of its limitations is critical to a successful riding strategy.

Your physical factors such as fatigue, stress, emotion, and body temperature can enhance or reduce your decision-making ability. Food, caffeine, alcohol, and medications can seriously impair your senses. Your body works on natural daily rhythms; some days are better than others, some times of the day are better than others. Ask yourself this: Are you more alert at 6 a.m. or 10 a.m.? Is your concentration better, or worse, when you're hungry? How focused on riding are you when you pull out into traffic after a long day of work? How focused on driving are *other* people when they pull out into traffic after a long day of work? The same limitations that apply to you apply to other road users as well—and while you can't control what others do, you can control what you do, and learn to recognize times of higher risk and adjust your strategy. That's what's so great about the mental challenge of riding: It's always there, it changes constantly, and there's

always room for improvement. Plus, it keeps things interesting.

Physical Skills—The More You Practice, the Luckier You Get

Physical skills make up only a small percentage of everyday riding, but when you really need them, they instantly become 90 percent of your survival. This is your second degree of separation. When something breaks through your mental barrier, as any hazard worth its weight will do, instinct, your adrenaline and instinct for self-preservation take over. At these moments, if your physical response isn't the correct one, you'll immediately need to rely on your third line of defense, your protective gear. But it doesn't have to go that far.

Controlled swerving or hard braking seem easy enough when you've got lots of room and lots of time, but when the pressure's on, do you really know how

they're done? And do you know the relationship between the two? Most people don't, although they think they do. Generally, in any situation, your first priority and best bet is to use the brakes to scrub off speed. Swerving is done when braking is no longer an option, or perhaps never was.

It's almost impossible to turn a bike without leaning it, and a swerve is really just two quick, consecutive turns. This means that to swerve, you need to lean the bike quickly, dramatically, and twice within a very short period of time. While it is possible (although slow and highly inefficient) to lean a motorcycle by leaning your body, to lean it quickly requires countersteering: forward pressure on the handgrip in the direction you want the bike to go. Example: if you want to swerve to the right, you press forward on the right handgrip. You actually (initially) point the front tire *away* from the direction of the intended path of travel. This seems backward to most people, and rightfully so. But like a mental strategy, it's a skill that can save your biscuit, so it needs to be *learned* and *practiced*.

The same holds true for braking. How many people really know how to use their brakes? Many riders avoid the front brake for fear of flipping over or locking up the front wheel and losing control. This is an uninformed and dangerous mistake. Under extreme braking on a two-wheeled motorcycle, the front brake accounts for 75–90 percent of the bike's stopping ability, and does so with mind-boggling authority. As the brake lever is squeezed,

weight is transferred to the front tire, increasing traction and stopping power, which allows the rider to squeeze still further. As more weight is transferred forward, more traction is available, allowing the rider *more* braking power. As the motorcycle loses speed and the front end decompresses, the weight begins to shift back toward the rear tire, allowing the rider more grip from the back. But by now the bike's stopped, and you're in first gear, ready to scoot out of the way of the car approaching rapidly from behind.

You knew about *that* because of your mental strategy—you were aware *before* you made your emergency stop of who was behind you, how far back they were, and how attentive they were. That, and you could hear the screeching tires. (Here, we see the first and second degrees overlap. To successfully complete this entire maneuver, you need both lines of defense.) Like swerving, this isn't something you can read about and then execute whenever you need to. It, also, needs to be *learned* and *practiced*.

An additional note on swerving and braking: they absolutely *must* be separated from one another—they cannot happen simultaneously. You can either swerve *or* brake, but not both at the same time. Each maneuver uses tremendous amounts of traction, and the traction available on a motorcycle is limited. When you push your motorcycle beyond that limit, the result is usually a crash. Here your mental skills again come into play: You must decide beforehand whether you will swerve or brake, or if you need to do both, *when* you will swerve and *when* you will brake, and how you will separate them to maintain control of your motorcycle.

A rider training course is the best place to begin exploring these skills. But remember that a one- or two-day class isn't nearly enough for you to know everything about yourself and your bike and your skills. Taking a class will give you an idea of what you need to know and some

Good countersteering is more a function of the duration of the handlebar input and not necessarily the force upon it.

Under hard braking, note where the rider's attention is focused.

When shopping for eye protection, take your helmet along with you and make sure whatever you're buying fits well underneath the lid.

brief practice in the applicable skills. After that, it's up to you to prepare yourself for the real world. Rider skills vary and decay over time, so they need to be practiced and honed constantly to keep them fresh.

Protective Gear—Have the Right Tools for the Job

Protective gear is your backup in case your first two lines of defense crumble. When all else fails and something finds its way past your first two barriers, what you're wearing is all you have left. This is your third degree of separation. It's technically a combination of the first and second degrees. Mentally, it falls under preparation. Physically, it protects you not only from the ravages of the pavement but also from elements such as heat, wind, and cold that can affect your ability to concentrate and operate the bike. (This third line of defense implicitly complements the first two). High-quality protective equipment that's designed specifically for motorcycling not only creates a layer of armor between you and the ground, it makes the first and second degrees of separation easier to manage, as well.

Let's start with the eyes. As your primary source of information for your riding strategy, your little round windows need unfailing protection from the effects of the wind and the sun. Sand, bugs, and rain can also wreak havoc with poorly protected eyes. When manufactured specifically for street riding, a face shield on a helmet is your best option, though goggles or tough safety glasses do the trick, too. Prescription

eyeglasses and sunglasses are legal in most areas and better than nothing, but they're not typically designed for use on a motorcycle and therefore are less desirable. They cover too little and let too much wind pass through. On windy days, dirt, insects, and dust can get through openings on the sides, bottom, and top of the frames and can cause you trouble.

Your head comes next, whether you like it or not. Wearing a good helmet will lower your risk. Not only will a properly fitting helmet help protect you from bashing your skull against the pavement, it will also protect you from the multiple stresses of the sun, the wind, and the cold. Dehydration and hypothermia can attack your body without your realizing it, and before you know it, your mental strategy and riding skills may no longer be available to you. Wind can be distracting, and wind noise can damage your ears. Rain, bugs, sand, and other airborne flotsam are just dying to find a chink in your armor and can make riding especially dismal to the unprotected head. While these lesser

If you don't wear glasses at all, consider buying two face shields—one for daytime and a tinted one for night.

hazards are not usually critical as far as injuries are concerned, they are especially critical to your attention span, and without constant, aggressive attention, your riding strategy is ineffective.

So what makes a helmet so special? Your brain does. Your brain is a delicate micro-processor in a liquid bath that can't take much physical abuse without shutting down. When your brain shuts down, the rest of your body tends to do the same. An improperly functioning brain makes even the simplest things difficult (e.g., alcohol), so it's critical to preserve it as much as possible. In a crash, a helmet is the best way to protect your brain.

The basic lid has two primary components: the shell and the liner. You've also got padding to keep it comfortable and a strap to keep it secure. The shell is usually some kind of plastic and the liner is usually expanded polystyrene—basically, Styrofoam. Picnic-cooler foam. The shell and the liner work together. The shell is designed to distribute the energy from a blow to the head over a large area, and the liner is designed to absorb that energy.

When the helmet is subjected to a trau-matic force like hitting the curb, a tree, the pavement, or another vehicle, the shell takes the impact force and spreads it out over the surface of the helmet. Let's imagine you hit a patch of sand at 5 miles per hour, wipe out, and hit the curb with the top of your helmeted head. Let's pretend the impact energy is 25 pounds per square inch, and the contact area of

the shell and the curb is 1 square inch. The shell then spreads out the impact force over an area of, let's say, 25 square inches. Now the force of the impact is only 1 pound per square inch, though it does now affect a larger area than the initial impact did.

Here's where the liner comes in. The expanded polystyrene is crushed and absorbs the impact force of 1 pound per square inch and acts as a buffer zone for your skull. You can imagine the same process at work when you jump into a haystack. To get an idea of how well this material works, imagine yourself on your knees, outside, making a fist, raising your fist high into the air, and with all your strength then bringing it down knuckles-first into a concrete driveway. If you had a big hunk of 1-inch Styrofoam handy, wouldn't you rather lay that on top of the concrete and then punch that? Sure, you might break your wrist if you hit the concrete hard enough, but you probably would have broken your wrist anyway. The Styrofoam protects your knuckles, hand, and wrist, and the negative effect of the cement is reduced greatly.

It seems that many, many people hate helmets. That's OK. Charles Darwin is alive and well, and he's out there driving around in a late-1970s Pontiac Bonneville with busted-out headlights and filthy windows, making lots of left turns against traffic.

Helmets that are DOT-approved do not limit peripheral vision while you're looking forward. The area you could normally see, peripherally, you can still see. As you move your eyes only, even-tually your field of vision will rotate to the point where the edge of the helmet does obstruct your peripheral vision. At this point, to see any further, the rider needs to turn his or her head.

Helmets don't block out important sounds from around you like engine noise, tire noise,

Check the squeegee carefully for bits of grit and dirt before washing your face shield with it.

Helmet face shields are notoriously hard to keep clean and scratch-free. So are plastic lenses of any kind. Paper towels and tissues will leave the surface scarred beyond recognition within a couple months. Scratched lenses present a safety hazard, especially at night. Use only soft, clean cloth to wipe your lenses. Microfiber towels work extremely well for keeping your face shield clean. Carry one moist towel in a plastic bag to wash the shield and a dry towel to wipe it off, and you can clean your shield any time and place, even if no water is available. In a pinch, gas station squeegees work well, provided you check the squeegee for grit that can scratch your visor.

Helmets don't cause neck injuries. Crashing does. Some dubious studies claim that the rate of neck injuries goes up in states that enact helmet laws. While this is probably technically true, what these studies fail to recognize from the statistics is that corpses don't complain about whiplash.

horns, or screeching brakes. Helmets reduce all sounds by approximately the same level. You still hear what you need or like to hear, just at a reduced volume. Even with foam earplugs, other vehicles and noises can be heard reasonably clearly.

To dispel a common myth, helmets don't cause neck injuries. Crashing does. Some dubious studies claim that the rate of neck injuries goes up in states that enact helmet laws. While this is probably technically true, what these studies fail to recognize from the statistics is that *corpses don't complain about whiplash.* All those riders who would've otherwise been dead (and probably with a neck injury up in biker heaven) are now alive to suffer the consequences of crashing. The unfortunate reality is that the helmet absorbs the impact and allows the rider to live, but like the broken-wrist-on-the-driveway example above, other injuries associated with the crash are still possible, and a good neck injury will last a lifetime. Best to wear the lid and use your mental strategy to avoid rear-end collisions.

A helmet will not make you invulnerable! Helmet manufacturers try to tell you that by not guaranteeing your head against injuries. If it's in good condition and fits properly, a helmet *will reduce* the severity of injuries in a crash. For lesser impacts, the helmet may prevent all injuries. For greater impacts, the helmet may not protect you at all.

Anyone who says helmets are uncomfortable has probably never tried one that fits properly. I challenge anyone who thinks helmets are uncomfortable to find one that fits and wear it for a couple hundred miles. They'll probably never go back.

Yes, helmets do get hot in the summer, but keeping cool in the summer is a problem for unhelmeted riders, too. If it's too hot to wear the protective equipment, it may be too hot to ride.

Decent helmets are *expensive.* You can get DOT-approved protection for as little as 100 bucks, but that's entry-level. High-quality helmets will run you upward of $400 to $700. What you're paying for after $100 is a combination of style, features, and comfort, which is arguably worth the dough. Buying an inferior helmet (such as a

phallic little cranium-cap with a head-shop DOT sticker) is a complete waste. They're not comfortable, nor will they protect you in a crash. And if you live in a helmet-law state and you get caught with a fake helmet, you've got Johnny Law to deal with, as well. If you have to wear one, get one that's built to the government's standard. Try one. Once you get used to it, I doubt you'll ever go back.

Helmets are designed to work *once.* When the shell compresses and distributes energy and the liner gets crushed, your lid will be less able to absorb impacts after that. Your risk of head injury will go up. It will still be less than if you're not wearing one at all, but it won't be as effective as it was when it was new. Dropping your helmet on the driveway can wreck it as well. Even if it's never been scratched, with all the wear and tear a helmet takes, as a rule you should replace it every two to four years. If your helmet is in good condition, you're less likely to be injured if you wear it. Period. Wear it, and maybe live to ride another day.

As always, you want to reduce injuries in a crash, but what else does good riding gear protect you from? How about sunburn, evaporation and dehydration, temperature extremes, sand, rocks, bugs, and rain? The motorcycle rider is vulnerable to the elements and needs a layer of protection.

To illustrate the injury-prevention properties of protective gear, let's imagine jumping out of the back of an unmoving pickup truck wearing nothing except your squid outfit: shorts, sandals, and a T-shirt. If the truck's not moving, it's no big deal.

But what if it's doing 5 miles an hour? At that point, I'd opt for some shoes—something that will support my feet when they hit the ground and provide good grip so I can stay upright. I don't want my toes exposed, and the sandals might slide around on my feet a bit. Leather-soled shoes might be kind of slippery, so I'll go with sneakers. Well, I am dropping from about 3 feet—high-top sneakers, then. (Protect the ankles.) I don't expect to tumble, so I'll just stick to the shorts and T-shirt for now.

How about at 15 miles an hour? It might be tough to keep on your feet. The shoes are probably still sufficient, but what if you can't land without rolling? Now I'm thinking something a little more sturdy than shorts and a T-shirt: maybe some thick, soft pants and a shirt. Just in case. Sweat clothes? Soft, but probably not good on asphalt. They might not stay put. I don't want my sweatshirt riding up on me and letting my bare back or belly hit the pavement. I need something with more structure, something sturdier. Denim? Now *that's* not a bad idea. A rugged pair of jeans and a jean jacket might be just the ticket in case my body has to hit the ground. That'll do. Maybe a pair of gloves, too. I fell on my hands and knees a lot when I was a kid. I seem to remember it hurt like hell.

Thirty miles an hour? I might be OK to *tumble* in denim, but what if I start sliding? That cotton would wear through in short order. At this point I'd rather have a second skin, a throwaway layer of leather covering my arms, legs, torso, feet, and hands. I'd want good leather, too, thick competition-weight leather and not that lightweight fashion leather they sell at the clothing stores. I want something that'll last for several seconds of crashing.

Sixty miles an hour? Now I'm trying to find a way out of it. Now I'm sure to get hurt without a good layer of gear. Now I

At 30 miles an hour, I'd be second-guessing my desire to leave the relative safety of a moving vehicle. My brain would be backpedaling. Maybe I could get the driver to slow down to about 5 miles per hour? Is there a good reason to be doing this?

want leather *and* extra padding. Padding at the shoulders, elbows, forearms, hips, and knees, all the pointy places. I also want something to protect my spine. I want sturdy boots and thick, sturdy gloves. I'm searching desperately for some soft-looking asphalt.

And so it goes. The higher the speed, the longer you'll tumble, or the harder you'll hit whatever it is you're tumbling toward. To survive a fall from a bike at any speed without injury, you need a second skin.

There are too many different varieties of riding gear to examine here. Leather seems to be the best and the most traditional. The guys who race wear it exclusively. Of course it seems to always be warm and it never seems to rain where they are. The synthetic gear seems to be a good compromise for everyday street riding. You don't get the protection from injury that leather provides, but then, you're not a trained athlete riding at 100 percent, either. The synthetic gear seems to hold up better in rainy weather, and is more versatile in dealing with temperature extremes. Generally speaking, it is also cheaper.

In theory, a properly executed mental strategy can protect you from everything. For those times when your brain can't save you, your physical skills and ability to control your motorcycle are your backup. But there will always be elements beyond your control—that's always true in life—and what your mind and skills can't protect you from, your riding gear has to. After the third degree of separation, all you're left with is blind luck, which is actually somewhat underrated—you'll find as you develop your riding strategy and physical skills that the more you practice, the luckier you get.

Each degree of separation can stand on its own, but is far more potent when combined with the others. Individually, each can bail you out of a bad situation, but together they create a formidable barrier to the risks associated with motorcycling. Each can be achieved through learning, study, and practice, but they need to be *learned*, they need to be *studied*, and they need to be *practiced*. No matter how long you've been riding, no matter how many near misses

The higher the speed, the longer you'll tumble, or the harder you'll hit whatever it is you're tumbling toward. To survive a fall from a bike at any speed without injury, you need a second skin.

No matter how long you've been riding, no matter how many near misses you've had, no matter how many miles you've traveled without crashing, there's still more to know.

you've had, no matter how many miles you've traveled without crashing, there's still more to know.

Three Degrees Part Two: Whose Fault Is It?

For a long time, I touted the theory that every motorcycle accident is the fault of the rider. I figured, "The rider is the one who's going to lose, so it's the rider who's got to look out for everybody else. The rider has to take responsibility for everything on the road." And I wasn't afraid to share the theory with my rider friends.

I got a lot of heat about it. What about a blowout? "Rider's fault." What if somebody pulls out in front of you? "Rider's fault." What if you slide out on a patch of sand? "Rider's fault." I took a lot of grief from a lot of people. What was so hard to understand about it? It was the rider's fault because it was the rider's job to avoid the situation in the first place.

I was wrong—to a point. I was inadvertently placing the *blame* on the rider, regardless of the circumstances. What I meant was that avoiding these situations was the rider's responsibility. My idea was correct. I knew what I meant, but I wasn't saying it properly. I wasn't trying to explain why the accident occurred; I was trying to show people how a smart rider could have avoided the situation, or could avoid the situation in the future. I was trying to take a positive approach, a (I hate this word, but it's perfect) *proactive* approach, to motorcycle crashes. (I promise not to use it again.) I wanted my friends to learn from their mistakes, to learn from others' mistakes, or better yet, *imagine* making mistakes, and learn from *them*. Being *reactive*—flaming, blaming, and regretting— is useless, and you spend too much time yelling, healing, and repairing your bike.

So at the time I didn't know it, but what I really meant was, *every motorcycle accident could have been prevented by the rider.* Every one? Every one. Here's an illustration:

Meet Veemax Vince. Vince is an everyday rider. (By that, I mean he rides every day.) Vince loves his bike. He uses it for commuting, transportation, traveling, and recreation. He likes the way he looks on his bike. He likes the way it makes him feel. He likes the power, and the wind. He smokes while he rides.

Oh yeah—Vince has never taken rider training, he doesn't use a riding strategy, and he doesn't wear protective gear. And he doesn't realize he's at a disadvantage. Vince genuinely thinks he knows how to handle his bike. Besides, he's ridden for two years without an accident. He knows what he's doing. Right?

One day Vince is on his way home from work. It's 4:30, summer, the sun's shining, and the traffic is the usual rush-hour variety. He's wearing penny loafers, slacks, a shirt and tie, and sunglasses. He's riding down Last Chance Avenue, an urban four-laner that has no median, stop lights every four blocks, and a 30-miles-per-hour speed limit. There's no parking on either side of the street, and gas stations, liquor stores, motels, and apartment buildings are spaced evenly apart. It's all very predictable. Vince is five minutes from work and five minutes from home.

Vince approaches a four-way intersection. He's got the green light and he's in the left lane. His plan, if you could call it that, is cruising straight on through at 30 miles per hour. On the far right corner of the intersection is a convenience store. In the right lane, in front of the convenience store, is a big delivery truck, parked illegally, with its flashers on. The truck is blocking Vince's view of the store's exit, but Vince doesn't realize it.

Sherry Cavalier, the woman who is trying to turn left out of the convenience store behind the truck, doesn't realize it, either. She takes a slug of her Coke, sets it down, looks left and right, doesn't see anyone coming, and pulls out—right in front of Vince. Vince's eyes grow as big as saucers, and he panics. He grabs a big handful of front brake and stomps on the rear. Sherry suddenly sees Vince, her eyes grow as big as saucers, and she panics. She slams on her brakes and stops directly in his path.

At this point Vince's ride is over. He slides, both tires locked and smoking, into Sherry's left-front fender at about 20 miles per hour. He is thrown from his bike, and he vaults over Sherry's hood and lands on the blacktop on his head and forearms.

Twenty minutes later, Vince is on his way to the hospital, in a coma, with a fractured skull, a broken hand, wrist, and collar bone. He's got multiple lacerations on his arms and chest, and a heaping helping of road rash. His bike is bent in half and lying in a pool of gas and oil. Sherry, after giving her tearful statement to the police, drives home with a bent front wheel and crushed fender, sipping the Coke she bought 40 minutes ago. It's still cold.

You've probably heard this story a hundred times. The names change, but the story remains the same. Neither driver was negligent, though both were arguably careless. Sherry will probably get a ticket for "Failure to Yield Right of Way." This will be little consolation to Vince's family, who has just found out that Vince is in the hospital and may or may not recover.

If either one of them had left the office five seconds earlier, this might not have happened. If Vince hadn't dropped his keys in the parking lot, this might not have happened. If Sherry had picked a fountain drink rather than a can, this might not have happened. If the light had been red, this would not have happened. If the delivery truck hadn't been parked illegally, this would not have happened. A million "what-ifs." If not Sherry, it would've been someone else—maybe not on that day, but someday. Eventually Vince was going to have to face this, or something like this. Vince was *high-risk*.

But was there something he could've done to prevent this? Was there a preemptive strike he could've used to lower his risks in this situation? Yes. There were a number of things he could've done.

If he'd been using a riding strategy, he would've been more cautious riding through the intersection. He would've

known the most dangerous place for a motorcyclist is an intersection. He might have slowed down, and covered his brakes and clutch to reduce his reaction time. He may have noticed the big blind spot created by the delivery truck, and slowed even more or adjusted his position to accommodate it. He might have devoted a bit more attention to focusing on the blind spot.

If he'd taken rider training, he'd have known how to use his brakes properly, and possibly might have been able to stop, or slow his bike enough to avoid the crash with a quick swerve.

If he'd been wearing a helmet, gloves, and a jacket, he might have gotten up, dusted himself off, and spent the next 10 minutes yelling at Sherry. Then he would've spent the rest of the afternoon lamenting the loss of his beautiful bike. He might not even have known enough to congratulate himself for using one or more degrees of separation, or to realize how lucky he was.

Any one of the three degrees of separation probably would've changed the outcome dramatically in Vince's favor. Had Vince been using all of them simultaneously, this accident likely never would have happened.

So learn the three degrees first; they'll save your biscuit hundreds of times before anything else will, except maybe luck. Once you master the three degrees, you'll probably want to learn more. It can be addicting. You'll *crave* more, and that's what the rest of this book's about.

Now we'll talk *finesse*.

Learn the three degrees first; they'll save your biscuit hundreds of times before anything else will, except maybe luck.

You Are Here

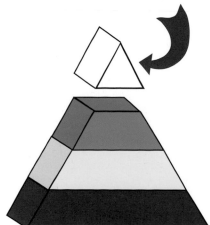

Before You Hit the Road:
- Plan your riding strategy.
- Get safety training, and practice what you learn.
- Buy the best gear you can find.
- Adopt the attitude that every crash can be avoided.
- Take it seriously. Vince didn't.

GETTING HURT 101

Motorcycling changed in 1981, and a man named Harry Hurt helped make that change happen. In fact, he may have set it all into motion. The then-current trends in motorcycling had built for many years and reached a peak. The numbers of motorcycles, motorcyclists, crashes, injuries, and fatalities had swollen steadily to a spike around 1980. After 1981, bikes, riders, and the associated death and injuries began to disappear. The numbers fell steadily and reached a bottom point around 1997. Harry Hurt and his team had a lot to do with that.

But the long and steady improvement in the safety of motorcycle riding didn't last forever. The challenge and image that goes along with motorcycling still attracts thrill seekers and those who fancy themselves more outlaw than accountant, more rebel than drone. The numbers are now on the rise again. Following a resurgence in motorcycling's popularity, we're again seeing more riders, more crashes, more injuries, and more fatalities. Shiny and indestructible youths have mind-boggling liters of horsepower available for about 150 bucks a month. Lots of riders who gave up riding 30 years ago to raise families are now throwing legs over motorcycles and trying to relive their youth. Many of them don't fare so well.

Like that crime dog with the big sniffer in the hat and trench coat, or that walking, talking bear always gravely reminding us about our responsibility when it comes to forest fires, I thought that this Hurt guy was a creation and not an actual person, a figure whose name or likeness summed up a group of like-minded individuals and gave them representation. Pat Hahn

But even given recent rises in fatality rates, the current fatality rates are only one-third of what they were in 1980. Giant leaps in knowledge, awareness, training, protective equipment, and motorcycle technology have all contributed to a much safer motorcycling environment in the twenty-first century.

The Hurt Study had a lot to do with that. This federally funded, two-year study laid out the who, what, where, why, when, and how of motorcycle crashes. The five W's told the government and motorcycle industry what the problems were and who needed help. The "how" told them exactly what needed doing. Not only did the authorities know who their audience was and what they needed help with, they were also given specific solutions.

My first exposure to Professor Harry Hurt was an article in a motorcycle rag when I was still very green. I'd learned to ride—taught myself, mostly—and wanted to learn more. I was hooked and looking for excuses to delve deeper into motorcycling. I was an enthusiast before I even knew what such a thing was. I had an itch and was looking for some way to scratch it.

There was a good deal of information to be found in motorcycle magazines. In one of the current events articles or a safety article or some such, someone made a reference to a big safety conference in Southern California. In the article, there was a detailed report about the speech delivered by one Harry H. Hurt.

At first, I thought it was a joke. Was it possible that a guy talking about motorcycle crashes could have a name like Hurt? I wasn't sure it wasn't someone pulling my leg. It sounded very tongue-in-cheek. Like that crime dog with the big sniffer in the hat and trenchcoat, or that walking, talking bear always gravely reminding us about our responsibility when it comes to forest fires, I thought that this Hurt guy was a creation and not an actual person, a figure whose name or likeness summed up a group of like-minded individuals and gave them representation. I pictured a ridiculous cartoon character, bandaged from head to toe in a Frankenstein body cast and sporting two black eyes. I guessed an ad campaign would go something like, "Don't do what Harry Hurt Does."

"Ha ha," I thought, "the safety guys have a mascot." Well, it turns out that part wasn't far from the truth.

Over time, I heard more and more about Harry Hurt and the unique, timely, and groundbreaking work he had done in motorcycle crash research. Hurt's team conducted a study to figure out why and how motorcyclists crashed, and recommend what might be done to reduce the numbers of injuries and fatalities. In Southern California over a period of a couple years, he and his team monitored the police scanner, raced on-site to reported motorcycle accidents, and evaluated the accident scenes. His crash reports were comprehensive and very thorough. His researchers were motorcycle enthusiasts, experts in motorcycle handling and dynamics, experts in injury mechanisms, and masters of on-scene investigation and follow-up. They talked to everyone they could at the scene, in patrol cars, and at the hospitals.

The knowledge gained from the Hurt Study was put to good use. Most of the safety courses being taught were developed or revamped to make use of the findings from the Hurt Study. Harry Hurt found many common threads in motorcycle crashes, and the Motorcycle Safety Foundation turned the information into specific skills that could be taught. Governments and industry leaders used the information to help educate the public.

The Hurt Study included 53 individual findings based on on-site studies of 900 accidents and reviews of 3,600 accident reports. In January of 1981, the findings were presented in their final form in the report *Motorcycle Accident Cause Factors and Identification of Countermeasures*, informally referred to as the Hurt Study. The conclusions were fascinating. Some of the conclusions were statistically less than significant and some are now a bit dated. But the facts are still very useful

The Hurt Study was published in 1981; the research was conducted in 1979 and 1980 and therefore still has a bell-bottom, 1970s feel to it. But the facts are still very useful today. Even some of the dated items, at their root, are still meaningful.

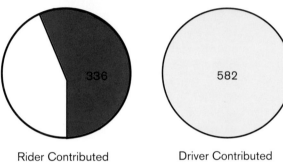

Minnesota Motorcycle Crashes

Year	Total Crashes	Single Vehicle	Multiple Vehicle
1981	3308	827	2481*
2001	1213	631	582

*estimated

Contributed Factors-2001 Multi—Vehicle Crashes

336 — Rider Contributed

582 — Driver Contributed

Assuming for argument's sake that Minnesota shared the Hurt Study's 25/75 ratio of single-vehicle to multivehicle crashes in 1981 in California, single-vehicle crashes in Minnesota have dropped only 24 percent, while multivehicle crashes have dropped a staggering 77 percent. Another more dramatic way to look at this is to see the fact that single-vehicle crashes dropped by about 200 incidents over 20 years, while multivehicle crashes dropped by nearly 2,000 incidents in the same time period. Motorcycle ownership also dropped dramatically during this period, but in 2001 ownership was again near the all-time high of 1981. Research into your own state's statistics might turn up something different.

Deep Thoughts

Remember, statistics do apply to everyone, but they don't apply to anyone. Maybe these findings may apply to you, but then again, maybe they don't. You have to decide.

today, and even some of the dated items, at their root, are still meaningful. The full report is several hundred pages and is available in printed form. The ordering information can be found at the end of this chapter.

This is an old study that definitely needs a successor. Look closely at the findings and learn from them. There are ways to incorporate all of this information into your riding strategy. It's also a good base from which to mentor another rider in the facts of life or bewilder the willfully ignorant.

Remember, statistics do apply to everyone, but they don't apply to anyone. Maybe these findings may apply to you, but then again, maybe they don't. You have to

decide. And rather than take what follows as typical, I recommend you dig around in your state traffic safety records and take a look at what's happening where you live right now. See Chapter 5 for help in finding this information on your own.

Hurt's Conclusions

Approximately three-fourths of these motorcycle accidents involved collision with another vehicle, which was most usually a passenger automobile.

Approximately one-fourth of these motorcycle accidents were single vehicle accidents involving the motorcycle colliding with the roadway or some fixed object in the environment.

OK, here we go: 100 percent of the accidents involved a rider crashing. In 1980, the biggest risk facing riders was deemed to be other drivers failing to recognize a motorcycle in traffic. Today, the ratio of multivehicle to single-vehicle crashes is now closer to one-to-one. About half of all motorcycle accidents involve single-vehicle crashes and half involve another vehicle. In fact, it now leans more toward single-vehicle events in some states. It's likely that motorists today are more aware of motorcyclists, or that motorcyclists are more aware of their limited conspicuity. The national motor vehicle code now requires that motorcycle headlights be on at all times. It could also point to the improved technology: startlingly colorful, high-quality protective equipment. The advantage of brightly colored gear is obvious when it comes to being seen by other drivers, but there also may be a correlation to the quality of the gear and the overall number of accidents. This is not to say that protective gear has any effect on the risk of a crash, but poor equipment and poor insulation from the environment can have negative effects on attention and perhaps even physical movement, so there may be some parallel benefits to modern protective gear.

If you look at the overall numbers in 1981 and 2002, you'll see that the multivehicle crashes have dropped far more than single-vehicle crashes. Considering that rider training, protective gear, and motorcycle technology made their greatest leaps forward in the same time period, it's not unreasonable to think it should be the other way around. For example, in multi-vehicle crashes in Minnesota in 2001, riders were attributed at least some of the blame for the crash about 57 percent of the time. Other drivers were found to have contributed almost 100 percent of the time. While this latter part may not be surprising, it is worthwhile to note that 57 out of 100 crashes could very possibly have been avoided simply by the rider's actions.

Maybe the campaigns alerting motorists to the presence of motorcyclists have had a greater impact than we think. Perhaps other drivers are not as big a risk factor as we have decided they are. Or maybe, after 20 years of motorcyclists trying desperately to become an accepted part of the traffic mix, Americans simply got used to seeing us around. How long did it take Americans to get used to compact cars? How long did it take us to get "safe" compact cars that worked as well as the enormous cars of old in a crash? Maybe half the problem was with the rider the whole time.

It should also be noted that recently the term "accident" has been supplanted in the safety community with the term "crash." Many people believe that the connotation of the word "accident" more closely resembles an act of God or fate rather than an unfortunate, avoidable mishap. "Accident" also connotes that the rider had no recourse or even chance of avoidance, and use of the term "crash" properly reflects some measure of the concept that rider responsibility and accountability, not luck, are at the heart of every incident. They're on to something there.

Vehicle Failure

Vehicle failure accounted for less than three percent of these motorcycle accidents, and most of those were single-vehicle accidents where control was lost due to a puncture flat.

Newer motorcycle tires are of the radial variety. Most of the tires during the Hurt Study were of a bias-ply type. Radial tires are far less prone to catastrophic failure. Nowadays, most likely, you'll walk out to

Go take a look around your local motorcycle junkyard. Count how many of the wrecked bikes, especially those with smashed front ends, have bald tires. Careful attention to detail and maintenance is all about attitude—the same attitude that applies to riding behavior.

your motorcycle in the morning to find the tire has gone flat, or you'll get a warning wobble.

Looking at how the numbers have changed over the last 20 years or so, it seems that maybe what's improved most is motorcyclists' conspicuity in the minds of other road users. Most riders think that other drivers are their biggest hazard. The statistics suggest this isn't necessarily so. When worrying about your safety, look first to yourself.

Another common form of rider error is the old "I had to lay 'er down," which is moron speak for "I don't know how to control my bike, so I locked up the rear brake and crashed on purpose."

Why did the chicken cross the road? Probably because it was hungry, thirsty, libidinous, or taking advantage of the cover of darkness to conduct business while the predators are at a relative disadvantage. Knowing when animals feed, mate, or move can help you avoid them in the first place. Spring and fall, dawn and dusk, near woods and water, and at night are all high-risk times for animal involvement.

But when choosing a cornering speed, do you consider the fact that you could blow a tire or throw a chain while heeled over and on the throttle? It happens only rarely, but if it should happen, could you control your bike in that situation? And if not, are you willing to accept that risk? If it ever happened to you, what would be the likely outcome?

Rider Error

In the single-vehicle accidents, motorcycle rider error was present as the accident precipitating factor in about two-thirds of the cases, with the typical error being a slide out and fall due to over braking or running wide on a curve due to excess speed or undercornering.

Two-thirds. That's statistically significant. These statistics are further verified by looking at modern fatality reports and crash statistics. Most commonly in a single-vehicle incident, a rider fails to turn tightly enough and runs off the road. If the rider realizes this in time, he or she may choose to overbrake and lock up the front or rear tire while leaned over to hasten his or her meeting with the pavement.

This is rider error in its most common form. Another common form is the old "I had to lay it down," which is moron speak for "I don't know how to control my bike, so I locked up the rear brake and crashed on purpose." The only place I've ever seen laying the bike down as the only option was on an old episode of "CHiPS" when Ponch

or Jon or some tan dude on a cop bike needed to slide his scooter under a half-open garage door in order to keep from being decapitated. But that guy was a professional stunt rider.

Road Hazards

Roadway defects (pavement ridges, potholes, etc.) were the accident cause in two percent of the accidents; animal involvement caused one percent of the accidents.

Compared to two-thirds, one and two percent don't seem like much, but it's still something to consider. In a state with 2,000 crashes a year, this still equates to 60 crashes caused by stuff like this. That's a lot. Since most traffic volume probably travels on urban surface streets, Hurt's findings here are probably pretty close to accurate today.

Where do you see most of the edge traps and bizarre pavement contortions? Highway, commercial, and residential construction sites. When do you see the worst potholes and the biggest patches of fresh sand? In the spring and after a good rainstorm, especially in awesome riding places like river valleys and mountains. But it does depend on where you ride. If you're a city commuter, you're in for one type of hazard. If you're a weekend country sport-tourer, you're in for another.

Understanding how weather and seasons affect roadways and construction can give you an edge. Understanding animal habits

We've all heard the "Officer, I just didn't see him!" argument. A good visual lead, constant scanning, and sensible lane usage and positioning can minimize the need for evasive maneuvers in the first place, and good motorcycle handling skills and training can further increase the chances that those evasive maneuvers will succeed.

on back roads at dawn and dusk, near rivers and forests, gives you an edge as well. The most enticing areas to ride a motorcycle are also prime habitat for deer and other fuzzy rodentia somehow compelled to jump out across your path at the slightest prompt. (For some good advice on night riding, see Chapter 7.) Maybe they're trying to kill those fleas once and for all.

The Other Guy

In the multiple-vehicle accidents, the driver of the other vehicle violated the motorcycle right of way and caused the accident in two-thirds of those accidents.

The failure of motorists to detect and recognize motorcycles in traffic is the predominating cause of motorcycle accidents. The driver of the other vehicle involved in collision with the motorcycle did not see the motorcycle before the collision, or did not see the motorcycle until it was too late to avoid the collision.

Hurt's findings should surprise no one who rides a motorcycle. We've all heard the "Officer, I just didn't see him!" argument. The only thing that has changed in 20 years is that it's somewhat more likely for today's motorist to say, "Officer, I just didn't see her!" The problem is that there are very few incidents in which a sensible person can justifiably remove all responsibility from the rider. A good visual lead, constant scanning, and sensible lane usage and positioning can minimize the need for evasive maneuvers in the first place, and good motorcycle handling skills and training can further increase the chances that those evasive maneuvers will succeed.

Deliberate hostile action by a motorist against a motorcycle rider is a rare accident cause.

As much as we'd like to believe that

they're out to get us, it's usually not true. It's unfortunately the unusual and startling cases that seem to get the most attention—and the best ratings—in the media. It's not a bad idea, though, to pretend for your own sake that they *are* out to get you. Pretend that they *will* act deliberately hostile. It's actually a pretty good idea for two reasons:

Reason 1: Your own safety. Riding with the attitude that everyone else on the road is deliberately trying to kill you will make you hyperaware of every other vehicle in your proximity. You'll also be extremely conscious of your position and your speed relative to the other drivers. Working hard to maintain a "me-against-them" state of mind, while also understanding that you'll likely be the only one riding in the ambulance, keeps you always in the correct defensive mode. In

It's you against the world.

that mode, it's easy to place yourself well out of reach of even the most unpredictable act of aggression, whether willful or just oblivious.

Reason 2: Making friends. If you pretend that everyone hates you and is trying to take you out, you might be

Some things never change. Your biggest risk for multi-vehicle crashes was then and is now another driver violating your right of way and causing a crash. You need to ask yourself, "Who does this? Where do they do it? Why do they do it?" The predictability of the answers might surprise you. (See Chapter 12 for those answers.)

It's good to play pretend. Pretend, for instance, that every other person is trying to kill when you're on your bike. Thinking like that, you start learning to position yourself better—way better. You also may have the urge to take the time to teach people—at work, at home, at school, wherever—why they shouldn't try to kill you.

Think of an intersection not as a place where two roads cross, but as a savage dagger thrust sideways into the harmonious flow of traffic.

If you had $10 million to build a contraption (like a giant mousetrap or a tiger pit) designed solely to unseat, unpretty, and unearth motorcycles and their riders, could you come up with anything better than this? Most multi-vehicle crashes happen in intersections just like this one.

Riding in the rain is something that should be practiced, even for those people who plan to never ride in the wet stuff. You never know if that helmet you're thinking about replacing leaks or fogs up when the humidity goes up to 100 percent, or if the rain suit that you bought but haven't used restricts your movements. Two hundred miles from home is a heck of a place to find out.

more inclined to change their minds about you. You might take the time to show people how nice you are, how normal you are, how friendly you are, and how vulnerable you are. Some people just don't realize that motorcyclists are not motorcycles, they're humans with friends and families and kids and homes and reasons to make it home in one piece. Feeling like a pariah, feeling like everyone's out to get you, and then taking steps socially to win people over, you can systematically begin reversing other drivers' desires to run you down.

Intersections

The most frequent accident configuration is the motorcycle proceeding straight, and the automobile making a left turn in front of the oncoming motorcycle. Intersections are the most likely place for the motorcycle accident, with the other vehicle violating the motorcycle right of way, and often violating traffic controls.

Think of an intersection not as a place where two roads cross, but as a steel battering ram smashing sideways into the predictable and harmonious flow of traffic. Intersections are the most dangerous places for motorcycles to travel. So it has been, and shall always be.

Conditions

Weather is not a factor in 98 percent of motorcycle accidents.

Yes, I'm really surprised by this one. I'll bet that 98 percent of the people who owned bikes in 1981 didn't ride in the rain. And I'd also imagine that most riders who choose to ride in the rain today probably have some experience doing so, and understand the added limits imposed on visibility, the rider's attention, and the bike's available traction.

In my experience as an instructor, I've regularly met people who were shocked that a motorcycle can actually be ridden in the rain (or snow) without falling down. It can be done, and should be practiced, especially by riders who do longer tours and stand a higher chance of being caught in a heavy rain. In fact, riding in the rain is something that should be practiced, even for those people who plan to never ride in the wet stuff. You never know if that helmet you're thinking about replacing leaks or fogs up when the humidity goes up to 100 percent, or if the rain suit that you bought but haven't used restricts your movements. Two hundred miles from home is a heck of a place to find out.

Most motorcycle accidents involve a short trip associated with shopping, errands,

Want to add two months to your riding season? Sell the car outright and buy yourself a commuter suit like this Aerostich Roadcrafter. The two months doesn't even count all the rainy days you'd otherwise drive the car—tack them on to the beginning and end of your riding season.

friends, entertainment, or recreation, and the accident is likely to happen in a very short time, close to the trip origin.

Professor Hurt posited that 90 percent of all motorcycle crashes happen within the first hour of riding and a whopping 50 percent happen within the first six minutes. Silly as it sounds, one of the smartest ways to circumvent the statistics is to never ride anywhere less than six minutes away. Want to reduce your chance

of a crash by 90 percent? Never ride anywhere closer than an hour away.

It seems the factors involved here are attention and concentration on the riding task. The transitions from house to bike, or bike to store, or store to friend's house, or work to home—those transitions are high risk. How long does it take to unwind after work? How focused on traffic hazards are you when you're mind is somewhere else? Six minutes of riding time after leaving the

Can you find the motorcycle in this picture?

Whose vision is more important to a motorcyclist, his own, or everybody else's? Put it this way: who's going to live longer, a legally blind motorcyclist riding around in traffic, or a motorcyclist with 20/20 vision riding around in traffic where everyone else is legally blind?

If you're spending less than three-quarters of your attention on what's ahead of you, you're overestimating the dangers coming from behind you.

house or work is the maximum time until impact for half the crashes. (This includes the two seconds you'll have between the time you see the left-turning car and the splat!) We'll explore this more thoroughly in Chapter 5.

Seeing and Being Seen

The view of the motorcycle or the other vehicle involved in the accident is limited by glare or obstructed by other vehicles in almost half of the multiple-vehicle accidents.

Conspicuity of the motorcycle is a critical factor in the multiple-vehicle accidents. Accident involvement is significantly reduced by the use of motorcycle headlamps (on in daylight) and the wearing of high visibility yellow, orange, or bright red jackets.

Whose vision is more important to a

motorcyclist, his or her own, or everybody else's? Put it this way: who's going to live longer, a legally blind motorcyclist riding around in traffic, or a motorcyclist with 20/20 vision riding around in traffic in which everyone else is legally blind?

We already understand that visibility is a key issue in multivehicle crashes. Lane positioning is critical to see other vehicles and for other drivers to see you. Glare from the sun is another matter, but good eye protection in the form of a tinted helmet visor or high-quality sunglasses worn inside your helmet will at least help you see the other vehicle, even if the driver can't see you. But as we'll see in Chapter 6, there is more than one approach to the concept of visibility, and what's most important may surprise you.

Since motorcycles are required to have a headlight on at all times, that's no longer as much of an issue as it was when the Hurt Study was published. However, daytime running lights on many cars have caused motorcycle headlights to be somewhat less effective in the daytime. Is there another way to set yourself apart from the crowd? Headlight modulators are legal and draw a great deal of attention, though some of that attention is welcome and some is not. Brightly colored clothing and reflective material is still a good idea and relatively inexpensive. Even a bright blue or red wind shirt over your bad black leather jacket, especially on morning and afternoon commutes, will enhance your chances of being seen. As a bonus, it's small enough so you can tuck it in your briefcase or satchel to retain your bad-seed leather-jacket look all the way from the parking lot to your office.

Motorcycle Collision Contact Areas

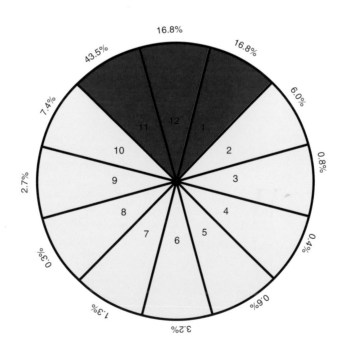

77.1 % From 11 to 1 O'Clock

These numbers show where the hazards were at either the moment the rider became aware of them or the moment they became hazards. Note how little of the risk comes from the peripheral fields, the ones so desperately sought after by those who think helmets are dangerous.

The typical motorcycle precrash lines-of-sight to the traffic hazard portray no contribution of the limits of peripheral vision; more than three-fourths of all accident hazards are within 45 degrees of either side of straight ahead.

Seventy-seven percent of all danger, according to Dr. Hurt, will come from the 10, 11, 12, 1, and 2 o'clock positions as the rider is traveling. The area behind you, where your typical loud-pipes-that-save-lives are aimed, accounts for about three percent of impacts. Sure, it's important to be cognizant of potential hazards from all areas of the clock face, but if you're spending less than three-quarters of your attention on what's ahead of you, you're overestimating the dangers coming from behind you.

Conspicuity of the motorcycle is most critical for the frontal surfaces of the motorcycle and rider.

Yeah, yeah, 77 percent, we remember. Considering what we know from the pie chart about where accidents are likely to take shape, it also stands to reason that others' ability to see the front of the bike is important. This includes the rider and his or her brightest-colored jacket and helmet. How about a really, really ugly orange or pink safety vest? A high-profile fairing that creates a good bit of reflective space can also make a rider more conspicuous. What about modifying the headlight?

Any effect of motorcycle color on accident involvement is not determinable from these data, but is expected to be insignifica nt, because the frontal surfaces are most often presented to the other vehicle involved in the collision.

Maybe true, but if the choice is yours, why not choose the more visible color? While a bright color might not help you avoid any crashes, could a subtle color increase your likelihood of a crash? Back then, when lots of people were unfamiliar with motorcycles and bikes were relatively recent additions to mass commuting, bikes probably all looked more or less the same from the front: tire, forks, round headlight, maybe a fairing or windshield. Today we have lots of ways to present ourselves to the world—why not take advantage of unique designs and colors and get some extra attention?

Reaction Time

The median precrash speed was 29.8 miles per hour, the median crash speed was 21.5 miles per hour, and the one-in-a-thousand crash speed is approximately 86 miles per hour.

If the median precrash speed is 30, then where do you think most crashes happen? The coming and going and to-ing and fro-ing make urban business areas and residential neighborhoods very unpredictable places to ride. We know that intersections are dangerous places. But there are different kinds of intersections. Do they represent different levels and types of risk?

The typical motorcycle accident allows the motorcyclist just less than two seconds to complete all collision avoidance actions.

Two seconds is less time than it takes to read this sentence. Are you comfortable with the idea that in the average hazardous situation, you have about two seconds to observe the problem, decide what to do about it, and then take steps to make it a nonproblem? It takes me 10 minutes at a restaurant to decide whether to have French toast or an omelet for breakfast. How can I decide about life and death in two seconds? I'd much rather that the average be about four seconds. Yeah, four seconds would give me plenty of time.

We know we can't change this two-second rule (though it may today be different of its own accord) but we can change how well we anticipate problems, how quickly we react to hazards, and how well we avoid them. How about avoiding the situation that creates the hazard in the first place?

The speed thing is interesting, though. Most people were going around 30 miles per hour (if my math is correct, that's 44 feet per second) when something jumped out at them, and had approximately two seconds between the time they detected the hazard and impact. That's 88 feet they had to work with. A trained rider can reduce speed from 30 miles per hour to a standstill in about *45* feet. Easily. Life is too short for a lack of braking skill to make it even shorter. Emergency braking is easy, but it needs to be learned and practiced.

We know we can't change the fact that we usually have only about two seconds to perceive and react to a hazard, but we can change how well we prepare for riding and anticipate problems beforehand. In other words, how well we prepare determines how well we use those two seconds. We can also change how quickly we react to hazards and how well we avoid them in the first place.

Who is more likely to crash due to a lackadaisical attitude toward drinking and riding? Who is more likely to crash due to a lackadaisical attitude toward death? Who is more likely to crash due to a false sense of security or familiarity?

Ask yourself the tough question. If I were to crash, what sort of crash would it be? Why would it occur? What mistakes would I have made that contributed to it? Examine what you know now, what you could do to try to prevent a crash. Is it possible that your behavior alone could prevent a crash from happening?

Mechanical Contributions

Fuel system leaks and spills were present in 62 percent of the motorcycle accidents in the postcrash phase. This represents an undue hazard for fire.

When motorcycles fall over, gasoline often comes out. I spill gasoline filling my lawnmower and have never caught it on fire. The genius that is modern cinema assures us that even big rocks will explode into noisome fireballs if they hit the ground hard enough, but don't you believe it. It takes flame or a spark to ignite fuel. I remember a crash scene in Phoenix once where the operator couldn't get up, but had the wherewithal to light up a cigarette. Fortunately, his bike was nowhere near him. Avoid smoking or playing with matches after any crash.

Vehicle defects related to accident causation are rare and likely to be due to deficient or defective maintenance.

I once heard a story about a group of riders who were enjoying lunch along the route of one of their favorite rides. As they were preparing to leave, a passer-by who had been enjoying some alcoholic beverages stopped to admire the late-model touring and sporting motorcycles. He was overheard to say "Doesn't anybody ride *junk* anymore?" The fact is that

people *do* still ride junk, but crashes aren't typically caused by bikes that fall apart while in motion.

That said, there's no excuse for a crash caused by neglect of the bike. Ignoring a worn or damaged whirlybit on a bike can be every bit as dangerous as ignoring the eyes blinking back at you from the bushes. Don't wreck an awesome curve by getting a busted chain caught up in the wheel.

Who's Crashing?

Motorcycle riders between the ages of 16 and 24 are significantly overrepresented in accidents; motorcycle riders between the ages of 30 and 50 are significantly underrepresented.

Who is more likely to crash due to inexperience, a younger rider or an older rider? Who is more likely to crash due to inattention, a younger rider or an older rider? Who is more likely to crash due to the speed of their reflexes? Who is more likely to crash due to the quality of their eyesight? Who is more likely to crash due to bravado? Who is more likely to crash due to peer pressure? Who is more likely to crash due to a lackadaisical attitude toward drinking and riding? Who is more likely to crash due to a lackadaisical attitude toward death? Who is more likely women still represent less than 10 percent of total riders, their overall numbers are lower, so their rates of injury and fatality vary greatly. Closer scientific analysis of this is necessary before we draw any real conclusions, but it bears mention. Women have joined the motorcycling society in terrific numbers, but the rate at which they crash and die is greater than that of men. Is it possible, or probable, that they crash for different reasons? I've overheard a learned friend and instructor say, "Women crash from inexperience. Men crash from testosterone." I think there may be some truth to that observation.

Craftsmen, laborers, and students make up most of the accident-involved motorcycle riders. Professionals, sales workers, and craftsmen are underrepresented and laborers, students, and unemployed persons are overrepresented in the accidents.

These may or may not be statistically relevant facts anymore, but they do point to an interesting link to the present. We see that three primary groups make up the lion's share of crashes. These same people probably also made up the lion's share of riders at that time. Interestingly, two of the three groups (laborers and students) that represented the majority of those involved in crashes were overrepresented in those crashes, but one (craftspersons) was underrepresented.

At the time the Hurt Study was done, motorcycling was still a popular transportation choice for the frugal and the young. As a college student in the late twentieth century, I can assure you that I had not the money, the adequately developed brains, nor the full-time job to keep me out of trouble. Draw what conclusions you will. As a motorcycle enthusiast and safety nerd, I now feel I know what I'm doing, but I'm still a hooligan at heart, and would beat the stuffing out of myself if I ever met me at that age. I can't believe I lived through it.

Currently, there is a growing attitude that street riding is a fun way to spend a sunny afternoon or a cool lifestyle image, rather than a means of commuting, transportation, or genuine recreation. This part-time attitude is arguably worse than the ignorant and

Year	Dominant Ages	Endorsed Motorcyclists	Registered Bikes
1978	21-29	185,000	151,000
1979	21-30	201,000	156,000
1980	21-30	222,000	157,000
1981	21-30	236,000	166,000
1982	21-31	246,000	159,000
1983	23-32	252,000	155,000
1984	24-33	256,000	153,000
1985	25-34	246,000	151,000
1986	25-35	275,000	141,000
1987	25-36	281,000	134,000
1988	26-37	286,000	128,000
1989	27-39	289,000	123,000
1990	28-39	292,000	120,000
1991	29-40	296,000	117,000
1992	30-41	290,000	116,000
1993	31-42	291,000	114,000
1994	32-43	293,000	113,000
1995	33-44	295,000	113,000
1996	34-45	297,000	112,000
1997	36-45	298,000	113,000
1998	36-47	301,000	118,000
1999	36-48	307,000	122,000
2000	36-48	312,000	132,000

If you look at the demographics over the last 30 years, you'll see that riders are getting older. Whether it's the same riders as 1971 still riding or the basic shift in focus of what motorcycles are used for these days, the majority age group among motorcyclists has increased in age like a rat through a snake.

In recent fatality reports, figures from 1981 still echo with a familiar ring. While younger riders are definitely still overrepresented, there is plenty of evidence that the 30 to 50 set is out and about, and getting killed on all varieties of bikes, especially big ones between 1,000 and 1,500 cc. Further, some statistics indicate that younger riders are crashing less and older riders are crashing more.

There are groups today that fill the same roles as craftspersons, laborers, students, professionals, and sales workers did in 1981. The current, growing attitude toward street riding as locomotion to and from the bar, and not as real transportation or genuine recreation, is changing who our prime crashers are. This part-time attitude is arguably worse than the ignorant and lackadaisical attitude undoubtedly shown by the laborers, students, and unemployed who were a big part of the problem back in the early 1980s. The biggest difference between those who crash and those who don't is how seriously they take motorcycling.

workers, and craftsmen are underrepresented and laborers, students, and unemployed persons are overrepresented in the accidents.

These may or may not be statistically relevant facts anymore, but they do point to an interesting link to the present. We see that three primary groups make up the lion's share of crashes. These same people probably also made up the lion's share of riders at that time. Interestingly, two of the three groups (laborers and students) that represented the majority of those involved in crashes were overrepresented in those crashes, but one (craftspersons) was underrepresented.

At the time the Hurt Study was done, motorcycling was still a popular transportation choice for the frugal and the young. As a college student in the late twentieth century, I can assure you that I had not the money, the adequatcly developed brains, nor the full-time job to keep me out of trouble. Draw what conclusions you will. As a motorcycle enthusiast and safety nerd, I now feel I know what I'm doing, but I'm still a hooligan at heart, and would beat the stuffing out of myself if I ever met me at that age. I can't believe I lived through it.

Currently, there is a growing attitude that street riding is a fun way to spend a sunny afternoon or a cool lifestyle image, rather than a means of commuting, transportation, or genuine recreation. This part-time attitude is arguably worse than the ignorant and lackadaisical attitude probably shown by the laborers, students, and unemployed who were a big part of the problem back in the early 1980s. The biggest difference between those who crash and those who don't is how seriously they take motorcycling.

The media have been falling all over themselves over the increasing rate at which baby boomers are dying on motorcycles. Statistics and studies bear that out. Yeah, lots of boomers are trying to get back into the youthful pursuits they gave up many years ago. The question is, which baby boomers are dying, and why? Is it as simple as riders returning to the sport after a lifetime of low-risk activity, or is there a fundamental change in the boomer sensibility?

Motorcycle riders with previous recent traffic citations and accidents are overrepresented in the accident data.

I wonder if the insurance industry knows about this? If they did, they'd probably find a way to charge you higher premiums if you show a lot of, uh, activity on your driving record.

The facts speak for themselves, and it's something to strongly consider when it

Your risk and your likelihood of a crash have everything to do with who you are at the time. It has everything to do with who you are and where you are—at what point in your personal evolution—when you expose yourself to the risk of riding. Think back to when you were young and invulnerable. What did you do then that you don't do now? What do you do now that you didn't do then? What was important to you then? What is important to you now? Pat Hahn

The facts speak for themselves, and it's something to strongly consider when it comes to your safety. If you've earned yourself multiple traffic tickets or if you crash a lot, you're probably riding too fast for conditions, riding over your head, or riding without the safety of yourself and others in mind. It doesn't take a rocket scientist to jack up your insurance rates.

comes to your safety. If you've earned yourself multiple traffic tickets or if you crash a lot, you're probably riding too fast for conditions, riding over your head, or riding without the safety of yourself and others in mind. It doesn't take a rocket scientist to jack up your insurance rates.

The motorcycle riders involved in accidents are essentially without training; 92 percent were self-taught or learned from family or friends. Motorcycle rider training experience reduces accident involvement and is related to reduced injuries in the event of accidents.

OK, 92 percent is what we can safely call "statistically significant." But in the late 1970s, motorcycle training was hard to come by. There simply wasn't much to choose from. Since then, rider training has evolved across the country in both quantity and quality, in no small part due to this particular finding. Now new riders have a way to learn correctly, and experienced riders have a nonthreatening and fun way to learn some new tricks (and relearn old ones). There are curricula for mopeds, sidecars, trikes, on-street training, you name it.

But what is it about rider training that makes such a difference? Skills like emergency braking, cornering (countersteering), and swerving are not instinctive and can rarely be learned without guidance. Many riders don't even realize they lack these skills until it's too late. If you don't know what makes a motorcycle lean, you'll never be able to swerve it in a hurry, when you really need to get out of the way.

But is that the only difference? Maybe not. A study in the 1990s in California suggested that crash rates for trained and untrained riders evened out after about six months. Using that, a person could draw the conclusion that after the initial high-risk period, the only thing between a rider and disaster was mental skills.

I learned to ride in a church parking lot; my mentor was just some guy I knew. His heart was in the right place, but looking back, it wasn't so smart. Mere minutes after learning the difference between the clutch and the brake, I was following him around like a fuzzy duckling on my very own bike. After 15 minutes of this level of instruction, we went from church parking

Skills like emergency braking, cornering (countersteering), and swerving are not instinctive and can rarely be learned without guidance. Many riders don't even realize they lack these skills until it's too late. If you don't know what makes a motorcycle lean, you'll never be able to swerve in a hurry, when you really need to get out of the way.

Swerving is really easy when you have all the time and all the space in the world to do it. But in an emergency, untrained riders generally do not know enough about the physics of swerving to know how to do it quickly when they need to. All it takes is a few minutes of instruction and lots of practice.

Interestingly, a recent study found that crash rates for trained riders and untrained riders seemed to even out after about five months of riding. This leads me to believe that the mental game is the critical key to survival on a motorcycle. The attitude that goes along with willingly taking a rider training course or willingly wearing a helmet, even when the law requires neither, is probably the same attitude that guides your riding style, choice of speed and position, and risk awareness.

lot to freeway. An hour later I was officially on my own. I can't tell you what I did to survive. I don't remember.

Almost every experienced rider who's taken my basic class came to me assuming they wouldn't learn anything. They were there as moral support for a wife or child, by order of the local constabulary, or to get the discount on their insurance. Most of them were happily surprised to find out that there were simple techniques that had never occurred to them and that they lacked more elaborate, critical skills they needed to learn and practice. The way their faces light up when they first try turning their heads and looking through the turn should be on the MSF logo. The way they come running over to tell me that, yes, indeed, that countersteering thing worked gives me the same superior know-it-all feeling I get when I help some lost tourist find his way. The MSF should

incorporate a light bulb over the head of the rider in its logo.

Logically, it would be irresponsible to attribute motorcycle crashes directly to a lack of training. To be fair, skills training is definitely a factor, but other factors, primarily the safety-minded attitude of the rider who takes the training, probably has as much of an impact on crash probability and injury reduction as the training itself. A good example of this is the Hurt finding that helmeted riders tended to be less involved in crashes than nonhelmeted riders. We all know that helmets are protective equipment only, and they have nothing to do with the likelihood of crashing or

If you had to share the same road every day with one vehicle and these were your two choices, which would it be?

avoiding a crash. (Well, if you consider the added comfort and concentration they afford, they may have a slight positive effect.) But the rider who chooses to wear a helmet is also probably a conscientious rider who is concerned with his or her safety. This overall attitude probably has more to do with crashing than training, helmets, and alcohol combined.

Look at it another way: if you were one of those cops who's really, really concerned with saving lives, who would you pull over if you saw them at exactly the same time:

A. A helmeted rider wearing full protective gear going 75 in a 55?

B. An unhelmeted rider wearing jeans and a T-shirt going 65 in a 55?

More than half of the accident-involved motorcycle riders had less than five months of experience on the accident motorcycle, although the total street riding experience was almost three years.

Jonah K., Momentum Motorsports Photography

The rider on top is going 80 miles per hour. The rider on bottom is going about 30 miles per hour. For whom do you fear most? Pat Hahn

This isn't surprising. When you get a new bike, it takes time to learn how it handles and performs. The familiarity you had with your last bike is gone, and you're starting from scratch again. You're distracted by the newness and the new feel of the seat, tank, controls, bars, pegs, sound, vibration, all of it. Riders need to understand that the first season on a new bike is at an elevated level of risk, and they need to adjust their riding style and space cushion accordingly. Be careful when switching to a larger or more powerful bike, as its performance may surprise you. Also, when switching to a smaller bike, be aware that the neck-snapping acceleration you were used to may be gone, and in it's place you may have more susceptibility to wind, bumps, and overzealous braking inputs. Practice and care are essential—know you're at low ebb in your skills when you are learning a new machine.

How long does it take to get used to riding a new (or new-to-you) bike? When you're getting used to a new machine, the extra bit of attention you need to become familiar with it has to come from somewhere. You unfortunately and undoubtedly take away from your hazard-avoidance strategy and concentration. When you don't have 100 percent of your attention and perception, your risk level goes up, and you need to adjust your riding to bring it back down again. This is the same for all riders, beginner or experienced.

Motorcycle riders with dirt bike experience are significantly underrepresented in the accident data.

This makes sense. Dirt bike riders generally start their motorcycling careers very young, and with some kind of mentor, guidelines, and protective gear as part of the equation. They understand well the value of preparation and the consequences of lapses of judgment. Their

How long does it take to get used to riding a new (or new-to-you) bike? According to the Hurt Study, about five months. When you're learning a new machine, the extra bit of attention you need to become familiar with the new bike has to come from somewhere. You take away from your hazard avoidance strategy and concentration. When you don't have 100 percent of your attention and perception available for riding, your risk level goes up, and you need to adjust your riding to bring it back down again.

Lack of attention to the driving task is a common factor for the motorcyclist in an accident. It was then, and still is now, a prime risk factor for any motor vehicle operator.

Riders with dirt bike experience were significantly under represented in the accident data. One can imagine that the ease, familiarity, and conditioning required to throw a dirt bike around, slide sideways, crash over, around, and through various obstacles, and general hand-eye coordination, strength, and balance is a tremendous advantage when it comes to handling a street bike in an emergency situation.

mental game is already half there. Plus, one can only imagine that the familiarity with throwing a dirt bike around, sliding and recovering from slides, bouncing over, around, and through various hard, wet, low-hanging, and prickly obstacles, and general hand-eye agility is a tremendous advantage when it comes to handling a street bike in a pinch. See Chapter 8 for a further discussion of this subject.

Lack of attention to the driving task is a common factor for the motorcyclist in an accident.

Not surprisingly, this is a common factor in all types of crashes. Motorists who are talking on the phone, applying cosmetics, reading, or dining while driving are all at risk for involvement in roadway unpleasantness. At least motorcyclists (unlike car drivers) are more or less unable to perform most of these tasks.

Remember, riding a motorcycle doesn't demand 100 percent attention. Riding a motorcycle doesn't demand any more attention than driving a car does. But riding a motorcycle safely, just as driving a

C'mon, guys—as if life isn't already short enough.

car safely, does require 100 percent attention. The point is so subtle you'll probably have to reread this paragraph. Know the difference and stick it into your bag of tricks.

Alcohol

Almost half of the fatal accidents show alcohol involvement.

True in 1980, but since then, the national average for motorcycle fatalities involving alcohol has dropped and now hovers around 45 percent. But that's an average. Some states have a much higher rate, and some, much lower. In Minnesota, for example, up until a couple years ago, the average hovered at an alarming *57* percent, with some years as high as 71 percent, over a 10-year period.

It is interesting to note the disparity in the rate of fatal alcohol involvement between car and truck drivers and motorcycle riders. Why are motorcyclists, on average, about one-third more likely than car drivers to die in an alcohol-related crash? While it's great that motorcyclists' rate is down to about 45 percent, the national average for car drivers is about 33 percent. Does this mean that motorcycle riders are a bunch of drunks?

But hold on. There's nothing inherent in motorcycles that makes us like to drink and ride. The two activities don't blend well at all. Riding isn't nearly as much fun when you have to stop and go to the bathroom all the time. Beer breath and whiskey belches are downright eye-watering when trapped inside a full-face helmet. Plus, while it's not impossible to open a beer while riding a motorcycle, it sure isn't easy. Sipping it at speed tends to get kind of messy. Neither is there a good place to keep beer cold on most motorcycles. There must be some other reason.

Could it be that the type of personality that is attracted to motorcycles is also the type of personality that is attracted to other "physical" forms of entertainment— like drinking? I know lots of people who don't drink alcohol at all. Almost all of them drive cars. But not everyone rides motorcycles. Motorcycling attracts a more adventurous crowd, a more self-indulgent crowd, a crowd with a higher level of risk acceptance. Simply said, I know a lot fewer motorcycle riders who don't drink than I do car drivers who don't drink. We're that type of people, I guess.

So maybe there are fewer nondrinking motorcyclists. This makes perfect sense. But might there be other reasons?

How about the recreational nature of motorcycling? Sadly, not every rider uses his or her bike every day. Dedicated commuters on motorcycles are few and far between. In the Midwest, our unofficial

> *Why are motorcyclists, on average, about one-third more likely than car drivers to die in an alcohol-related crash? Riding isn't nearly as much fun when you have to stop and go to the bathroom all the time. Beer breath and whiskey belches can be positively brain-fogging when you seal them up inside a full-face helmet. Plus, while it's not impossible to open a beer while riding a motorcycle, it sure isn't easy. We motorcyclists must be a bunch of drunks.*

Notice that the last part doesn't say, "Be Sitting in a Stinky Bar While All the Real Riders Are Out Motorcycling."

Chapter 2

Combine an outdated casual approach to drinking and driving common a generation ago with the requisite higher level of risk acceptance motorcyclists have, then throw in the basic modern recreational nature of motorcycling, and it's not difficult to figure out why alcohol-related fatalities are more common among motorcyclists than among car drivers.

start of motorcycle season is Memorial Day weekend. Our unofficial end of the season is Labor Day weekend. Many bikes only come out on the weekends and evenings in between. Many more still only come out on sunny and perfect weekend days. (We'll note in Chapter 5 that this is when most of the fatal crashes happen, too.) Those riders use their bikes for fun, entertainment, and relaxation.

What else do people use for fun, entertainment, and relaxation? "I love my motorcycle. I love hanging out with my friends. I love drinking beer. I love drinking beer with my friends. I think I'll combine everything together, and I'll have the most fun a person could possibly have!" Put it on your tombstone, pal.

OK, we've got a group that likes their drink and a group that likes to recreate. Can there possibly be anything else?

It makes a good deal of sense to look at who's actually riding the motorcycles out there. The core motorcyclists today are also the ones who grew up and socialized in a time when drinking and driving wasn't such a big deal. The age group, at least in my own home state, that holds the lion's share of motorcycle endorsements is the 36–48 group. Interestingly, this group has recently become overrepresented in fatal crashes, along with the related larger-displacement motorcycles and higher speeds. It could very possibly be that they just don't take drinking and riding (or driving) nearly as seriously as the rest of society.

Put it this way: a 36 year old in 2002 would have graduated from high school in about 1984, just before the time public schools and groups like MADD and SADD became actively, vehemently involved in teaching people not to drink and drive. It was in the mid-1980s that drinking and driving started becoming socially taboo. Many men and women born before 1970 probably remember the days when drinking and driving was a fact of life. They probably remember the time when an open beer in the car was no big deal. I know I certainly do. Driving after drinking was common. Drinking and driving was just as ridiculously stupid then, but it wasn't considered the social catastrophe that it is today. Many of these people on the long side of Generation X and into the boomer

generation probably remember stories about how being nice to the cop who pulled you over meant you'd get a ride home to sleep it off rather than a ride straight to jail.

On the other hand, kids in the twenty-first century are taught early and thoroughly about the stupidity of drinking and driving and the intelligence of using a seatbelt. There is a whole generation and a half who never got it, and probably never will.

Combine a middle-aged casual approach to drinking and driving with the overall higher level of risk acceptance motorcyclists have, then throw in the recreational nature of motorcycling, and it's not difficult to figure it out why alcohol-related fatalities are more common among motorcyclists than among car drivers.

Motorcycle riders in these [alcohol-related] accidents showed significant collision-avoidance problems. Most riders would overbrake and skid the rear wheel, and underbrake the front wheel, greatly reducing collision avoidance deceleration. The ability to countersteer and swerve was essentially absent.

Oddly enough, riders unimpaired by alcohol have similar problems. Choosing to not consume alcohol doesn't give you these skills, but consuming it can take them away—if you ever had them in the first place.

This type of finding is a primary factor in the purpose and structure of the MSF basic and experienced curricula. The skills indicated here—braking, swerving, and countersteering—are taught and practiced, as are cornering and tight-turn techniques. They're not skills that come naturally or instinctively to the motorcycle muddlers of the world. There is an outside chance that a conscientious rider could learn these things independently of training, but then we're stepping back into a world of good motorcycling attitude again. Those riders are way ahead of the game, whether they realize it or not. They seek the answers to questions they haven't even considered, and use the answers to solve problems they maybe didn't know existed.

Lots and lots of riders muddle through life, imagining they're using their body weight to lean the bike. They never realize they're countersteering, and if they don't

You know what kind of risk this driver presents. What is it going to take for him or her to surprise you? The rider who's least likely to crash is the one who's least likely to be surprised out there.

Hurt suggested that an alarming number of accident-involved riders, when faced with an impending disaster, did "nothing" to avoid it. Were they not even aware of the hazard, or did they not believe it was a threat, or did they want to avoid it but simply didn't know how? Could it be they fixated on the obstacle and froze up?

realize it, they can never do it on purpose. The same mistake applies to riders who don't understand the weight shift involved with heavy braking, during which most of the stopping power comes from the front tire.

Hurt also said that an alarming number of accident-involved riders, when faced with crash-causing hazards, did nothing to avoid them. This begs a great number of questions. Were those riders not even aware of the hazards, or did they not believe the hazards were threats? Did they want to avoid them but simply didn't know how? Could it be they fixated on the obstacles and froze up?

Or is it possible that it was a built-up resistance to the drama that a hazard presents? Can a rider who's gone a long time without a mishap simply become too cavalier about the whole thing? When someone has had 10 people almost pull out in front of him or her, but then catches his or her mistake and stops short, how loud does the alarm sound when right of way-violator number 11 pops into his or her path of travel? What if you, as a rider, had successfully lucked out of 100 bad situations, each time with very little adjustment on your own part? Would number 101 be any different? In the words of a good friend, they're called "accidents" because you

don't intend for them to happen. If that were the case, you'd call them "on-purposes." Crashes are *always* a surprise. One minute you're riding and the next minute, you're not. If they weren't surprises, they wouldn't happen, right? The difference between a rider and a good rider is how often they're actually surprised in traffic.

Other Conclusions

Passenger-carrying motorcycles are not over represented in the accident data.

Of course, when your typical accident-involved rider doesn't know how to countersteer, brake, or swerve anyway, what difference would a passenger make? Having the added weight and higher center of gravity wouldn't affect the motorcycle's handling if you don't know how to handle it in the first place.

I've been blessed (and cursed) with the opportunity to study fatal crash reports in Minnesota, the narratives that describe the incidents, the factors, the road conditions, the outcomes. It's a gruesome task, but not without its merits in the end. Based on the fatality reports I've studied, crashes involving riders with passengers often meant death or serious injury for the passenger, regardless of the severity of injury to the rider.

Crashes are always a surprise. One minute you're riding and the next minute, you're not. If they weren't surprises, they wouldn't happen, right? The difference between a rider and a good rider is how often they're actually surprised in traffic.

Personally, I think it's a lot easier to keep an extra eye on a car full of kids slugging Mountain Dew or a van full of octogenarians on their way to Bob's Bingo-and-Bran Buffet than to try to guess the knowledge level of every parent-age driver on the road.

The drivers of the other vehicles involved in collision with the motorcycle are not distinguished from other accident populations, except that the ages of 20 to 29, and beyond 65 are over represented. Also, these drivers are generally unfamiliar with motorcycles.

Here we are afforded an opportunity to stereotype entire generations. Back in 1980, a lot of motorists were still unfamiliar with motorcycles. Many, unfortunately, are still unfamiliar with motorcycles. While it's evident that drivers of all ages can be involved in accidents with motorcyclists, it's not a huge leap to expect that elderly drivers' vision, attention, and reactions are fading into the sunset. Additionally, it's not a stretch to ascribe higher risk to teenage drivers, who are only just learning to drive, only just learning about sex, only just learning how to drink, and only just learning how to work eight hours a day. Such riders could pose a higher risk than drivers who are accustomed to doing these things. An interesting fact, too, is that teenage drivers today represent only about 7 percent of licensed drivers, but are involved in about 15 percent of reported crashes, motorcycle or otherwise. It seems age and experience *are* factors in accident causation.

But look at it another way: if you had your choice, which age groups would you choose to be unfamiliar with motorcycles? The 20–29 and 65 and older groups, or the 30–64 group? Take a look at who's got all the licenses, at who owns all the motor vehicles—and who's involved in all the crashes—and decide for yourself. Personally, I think it's a lot easier to keep an extra eye on a car full of kids slugging Mountain Dew or a van full of octogenarians on their way to Bob's Bingo-and-Bran Buffet than to try to guess the knowledge level of every parent-age driver on the road. Remember, a bird in the hand is worth two gift horses in the mouth.

The large displacement motorcycles are under represented in accidents but they are associated with higher injury severity when involved in accidents.

This is changing in the late twentieth and early twenty-first centuries, but I can see where in the past, older, more experienced, and more affluent riders would more likely ride larger bikes. The younger crowd back then probably rode smaller, less expensive, and less powerful bikes to putter around on, to get back and forth to school or the café, or for general low-cost entertainment. Today, older doesn't necessarily mean more experienced, as a lot of people in their maximum-income years are learning to ride for the first time or returning after a long hiatus.

Today, larger bikes are the motorcycles of choice among the returning-to-motorcycling crowd and those who have ridden a long time and have made many upgrades. They also appeal to new riders who are eager to ride what their friends ride and to be immediately part of the group. Really large bikes— those monstrosities that boast neither form nor function— seem to find themselves in the hands of the something-to-prove crowd. The only one of these scenarios that makes sense is the experienced-rider upgrade. All the others smack of an uninformed method of quickly getting in

How old were you when you first realized how unbelievably ignorant you used to be? Somehow, most of us make it to adulthood and breeding age, but should we really trust someone who can't even put his cap on straight behind the wheel of a two-ton battering ram?

He probably knows what he's doing, but just what is he trying to say with his choice of ride?

over your head. National statistics bear this out—more older riders are dying on larger bikes than in past years. However, the media love to tell us that older riders are dying in greater numbers, although the reality is that they're still underrepresented in crashes, and younger riders are still overrepresented. The rate at which older riders crash is indeed increasing, and the rate at which younger riders crash is now decreasing, but the disparity still remains—younger riders are more likely to crash.

It's not difficult to see the relationship between speed and injury severity. If I were going to willingly smash fender-first into a brick wall, I would definitely prefer to do it at 30 miles per hour as opposed to 60 miles per hour. One way to decrease injury severity is to decrease speed. The state of Minnesota found the same thing after the speed limits went up here a few years ago—we saw more fatalities and greater injury severity on those roads where the limits went up.

Larger-displacement bikes, heavier and able go faster more easily, lend themselves to greater speed and greater injury. From experience, I understand that a bigger bike makes less racket, takes less effort, and simply gets up and goes—and stays there—

far easier than a small-displacement bike. Riders simply don't feel as if they're going as fast as they are, and the higher average speed multiplied out into everyday crashes will easily give you a higher rate of death and injury. I do concede the possibility that brakes and braking knowledge back then made it quite a bit more difficult to stop or slow a moving bike, but do we have that excuse today?

This study was conducted when there were numerous smaller displacement motorcycles available. Today's marketing experts from the major manufacturers have decided that Americans won't buy street motorcycles smaller than about 500 cc. While there are a few bikes available in that range, the 600-cc and larger market in sport bikes has exploded (up to the 1,300-cc Suzuki Hayabusa). The rush toward big-displacement engines is even more rampant in the cruiser segment, with its big-bore motorcycles and haughty disdain of any powerplant displacing less than 90 cubic inches.

Motorcycle riders in these accidents were significantly without motorcycle license, without any license, or with license revoked.

The skills necessary to gain a license endorsement are *exactly* those skills critical to crash avoidance and motorcycle control.

This bike has a purpose. Make sure that the purpose of you bike matches the reasons you ride, and if those reasons are wrapped up in the purpose of the bike, think a little harder about why you ride in the first place.

If you like high speed, be prepared for more severe injuries. If you like to travel quite a bit faster than those around you, you should be prepared for more crashes, too. The same goes for those who ride a great deal slower than the rest of traffic. I'll come back to this in Chapter 12.

While the relevance of riding around little cones and through 90-degree corners on the street may be debatable, the skills measured during a motorcycle riding exam are very real— overall control, balance, reflexes, knowledge, and efficiency. If a rider can't successfully stop or swerve quickly at 15 miles per hour, it is unlikely he or she could do it at 50 miles per hour. If a rider can't corner successfully at slow speeds, how can he or she possibly corner at high speeds, or in the dark, or with a passenger?

This finding is not nearly as important as it was before the MSF and state rider training programs spread their fingers across the country. Now that many states waive the riding test for those who've passed an approved safety course, we see an influx of riders who were either too busy to schedule a license exam or unable to pass it with their level of skill. Riders acquiring and renewing their motorcycle permits for years and years (I had a student who rode on a permit for more than 10 years!) or simply riding unlicensed over the years are far more common than I would have thought, but their numbers have diminished dramatically. Still, the unlicensed riders who still exist are at high risk of incident, not only from the lack of

skills and training, but also from the ignorance and careless attitude that probably accompany the unendorsed rider. If you are an unlicensed rider, no matter how many years or miles you have under your wheels, it's time to take that test and earn it. If you can't, there is probably something you should know.

Motorcycle modifications such as those associated with the semichopper or cafe racer are definitely over represented in accidents.

So, are we talking changes in physics or changes in disposition, here? Changing the basic geometry of your motorcycle will not necessarily make you crash. It will, however, change the handling and performance of your motorcycle. Be aware that even small changes in where your motorcycle's triple-tree grabs the forks can significantly change handling characteristics. Changes in the wheels or tire profile can have dramatic effects on the timing, predictability, and feel of cornering. These characteristics may be instantaneous and constant, or they may only exhibit themselves at highway speeds. The results could be enhanced performance, better feedback, a low-frequency steering wobble, or the tankslapper to end all tankslappers.

When the purpose of a bike is changed, through aftermarket hoo-ha or metal-shop magic, from a mode of transport or recreation to an accessory to make its owner look cool or a device for getting its rider somewhere really, really fast, the owner's attitude has probably shifted away from self-preservation and into something else. Such aggressive modifications typically result from a focused project designed to enhance performance, fit an image or a lifestyle, or to blend in with a group. Riders obsessed with street performance, or those who are more concerned with the appearance of their bike than its handling or stopping abilities, should think hard about why they ride in the first place. Maybe their interests are in the racetrack, or in building show bikes, rather than putting their lives on the line for the sake of image.

Injury severity increases with speed, alcohol involvement, and motorcycle size.

Notice that Hurt doesn't suggest these things are related to crashing.

All three of these factors are completely within the rider's control, although the relationship between motorcycle size and injury severity is more than indirect. I'm going to explore the relationship between

speed and injury severity more thoroughly in Chapter 4, but the long and short is, the faster you go, the worse you get hurt in a crash. That only makes sense. Not many people would choose to crash at 60 miles per hour if they had the option to crash at 30 miles per hour, right? Alcohol's involvement is, of course, elementary—impairment leads to poor judgment and increased risk taking. Bigger motorcycles get up and go much more easily, and generally don't make as much noise or need to huff and puff to stay there. Riders of bigger bikes probably feel as if they're going a lot slower than they actually are, especially after a few brews.

Regarding alcohol, if you like to drink and ride, you're probably not reading this book. If like to drink and ride and you are reading this anyway, the best of luck to you. But please note, riding a motorcycle is difficult enough without taking away your attention, vision, perception, judgment, balance, motor skills, and inhibitions. Everything you read in this book can't even touch the margin of safety you'll gain by separating drinking from riding.

What Happens When You Crash?

The likelihood of injury is extremely high in motorcycle accidents; 98 percent of the multiple-vehicle collisions and 96 percent of the single-vehicle accidents resulted in some kind of injury to the motorcycle rider. Forty-five percent resulted in more than a minor injury.

Half of the injuries to the somatic regions were to the ankle-foot, lower leg, knee, and thigh-upper leg.

If half of the injuries are to the legs, where are the other injuries likely to occur?

By their nature, motorcycles leave your "cheese in the wind" and are likely to result in higher rates of injury when crashed. This is an important point in your concern for your own safety. When you're out there on your bike, you're not only battling the likelihood of a crash, you're simultaneously battling the fact that if you do crash, you're almost certain to be hurt. To get an accurate estimate of your risk, it's necessary to take into account both the likelihood of a crash and the surety of an injury, probably one that will curb your

If you knew that you were going to crash today, how fast would you ride? If you were told in advance that this was definitely your day to kiss the pavement, how would you prepare for it? Which roads would you take? What would you wear?

If you like to drink and ride, you're probably not reading this book. If you like to drink and ride and you are reading this anyway, the best of luck to you. But please note, riding a motorcycle is difficult enough without taking away your attention, vision, perception and judgment, balance, motor skills, and inhibitions. All the concepts in this book, executed perfectly, won't do as much for you as the simple act of separating drinking from riding.

It's fairly difficult to believe that riders have an 80-plus percent likelihood of being injured in a crash. It could be 80 percent, it could be more, it could be less. The reason it's hard to believe is that statistics can only tell us about reported crashes. How many of your crashes didn't involve a police accident report?

While there's no guarantee, wearing good gear can take the teeth out of a serious mistake on the road. Get the best you can afford.

riding for a while. I will attempt to help you do that in Chapter 4.

Since the time of the Hurt Study, the rate of injury for motorcycle riders has decreased, although only slightly. An average rider still has an 80 percent or greater likelihood of an injury in a crash. This could be worse or better than we believe. I strongly suspect that a tremendous number of motorcycle crashes go unreported, especially single-vehicle crashes. Put it this way: Of all the times you have crashed your bike, how many of those involved a police report?

Let the suit take the damage. You can always buy another one, and repairs are a lot cheaper than skin grafts.

The use of heavy boots, jacket, gloves, etc., is effective in preventing or reducing abrasions and lacerations, which are frequent, but rarely severe, injuries.

While there are absolutely no guarantees, wearing good gear can take the pomp and circumstance out of a serious mistake on the road. There are lots of ways to protect yourself—your mind is the best way—but get the best gear you can afford anyway.

The scientific reference to road rash doesn't do it justice. Imagine taking sandpaper or a file to several areas of your body and grinding them down to the soft

flesh underneath the skin. Sounds awful, doesn't it? It gets worse. My understanding is that the worst part is when nurses clean out the wound by scrubbing the abrasion with a stiff-bristled brushlike item. Rather not feel the pain? Wear the gear. It's not guaranteed, but it can help keep a mishap from changing your life.

The motorcyclist in at least 13 percent of the accidents sustained groin injuries. These were typified by multiple vehicle collision in frontal impact at higher than average speed.

Here we see natural selection at work. Even a minor crash, correctly executed, can send you hopping into the land of severe testicular trauma, another reason to watch your speed and practice your braking.

It's not surprising that groin injuries are common in frontal motorcycle collisions. You're straddling a piece of heavy machinery, and when it stops suddenly, the parts of your body in contact with it have to stop too. Don't expect your arms to lever you safely away from the pointy edge of the gas tank. Consider sitting farther back from the tank.

Helmets and Eye Protection

Seventy-three percent of the accident-involved motorcycle riders used no eye protection, and it is likely that the wind on the unprotected eyes contributed to impairment of vision, which delayed hazard detection.

For the love of Pete, how stupid *were* people back then? My eyes get sore when I play nine holes of golf without my Ray-Bans on. Fortunately, with eye-protection laws these days and the availability of quality visors and face shields for helmets, the lack of eye protection is not as much of an issue.

We must assume that governments now require riders to protect their eyes because this reduces the number of crashes, especially multivehicle crashes. If someone, someday, found that the use of a helmet also reduced crashes—especially those that involve damage to another person's property—you can bet that mandatory helmet laws would be on the legislative docket.

It's also fortunate that sunglasses don't infringe on adults' right to choose the way

After a day of riding, who's more likely to notice the surface hazard at twilight? My money's on the helmetless guy.

helmets do. Nearly everyone agrees that it makes sense to wear something over your eyes while riding. Even Wile E. Coyote wore goggles on his rocket sled. Eye protection, any eye protection, likely reduces the number of crashes involving another motorist, sparing members of the public that unnecessary inclusion of a motorcyclist in their lives.

Remember, a motorcycle rider's sole source of useful hazard-detection information is visual. Don't compromise your eyes, ever. Along with a defensive riding strategy, vision is your absolute first priority. I'd rather see a rider with good eye protection and no protective gear than one with a good helmet and riding suit with no eye protection.

Approximately 50 percent of the motorcycle riders in traffic were using safety helmets but only 40 percent of the accident-involved motorcycle riders were wearing helmets at the time of the accident.

This is valuable, valuable data. Hopefully it continues to be ignored by the lawmakers.

Here you have proof that not only did helmeted riders suffer less in crashes, they simply *had* fewer crashes. This, again, exemplifies that it's the *attitude* that accompanies helmet use that's probably

the primary factor in crashes and crash avoidance. The rider who wears a helmet is conscious of his or her safety and takes other measures to ensure it, as well. Wearing a helmet can also make you more comfortable and alert. Comfortable, alert riders are better able to carry out hazard detection and avoidance techniques.

We absolutely cannot ignore, however, that this 50/40 percent helmet finding came from Southern California between 1979 and 1980, and that it's only completely relevant then and there. While it wouldn't be totally unreasonable to assume that helmet use was nearly the same across the country as it was in California, and it wouldn't be wrong to assume that the more safety-conscious riders back then crashed less, comparing helmet use 20 years ago to today is like comparing apples to airliners.

Modern helmet technology gives us a lightweight, tested, vented, and comfortable piece of fairly slick-looking equipment. Face shields are far better, as well. The helmet of the late 1970s took away from the rider's vision and was relatively ineffective, heavy, ugly, uncomfortable, and—to hear it told by riders far older and more experienced than

Remember, a motorcycle rider's sole source of useful hazard-detection information is visual. Don't compromise your eyes, ever. I'd rather see a rider with good eye protection and no protective gear than one with a good helmet and riding suit with no eye protection.

If helmets are injury-prevention devices, why did the riders who wore them crash less?

It's very simple: If it's too hot to wear the gear, it's too hot to ride the bike. If it's too short a trip to wear the gear, it's too close to ride the bike. And don't forget, half of all the crashes in Hurt's study happened within the first six minutes of the ride. Don't ride anywhere less than six minutes away.

I—stinky. Adequate full-face helmets today are quite a bit cheaper than their disco-era counterparts, as well. Even the cheapest DOT-approved helmet, while lacking in style, comfort, and features, is still effective in reducing head injuries and probably twice as comfortable, half as heavy, and has a much larger field of vision than its ancestors 20 years ago. It's not a big stretch to assume that helmet wearers were a sight less likely to be involved in a crash, but it should be noted that to wear a 1970s-era helmet, you had to be pretty dedicated to your own safety, and willing to put up with a lot to gain that extra margin of safety.

But let's take a slide down the slippery slope, just for argument's sake. If we buy into the fact that the safety-conscious attitude that goes hand in hand with the decision to wear protective riding gear also reduces the risk of crashing in the first place, would a mandatory helmet law reduce the number of crashes? I think it would. A national helmet law would drive the worst of the safety-malconscious riders out of motorcycling altogether—those riders who would choose to give up riding rather than wear a helmet—and thereby reduce crashes by reducing the number of poor attitudes out there on motorcycles. I don't mean by this to suggest or even give an inkling of support to any sniff of a helmet law. I think riders should decide what they wear. But I believe enacting one would have exactly the benefit lawmakers hope for—reduced head injuries—and would also have an indirect benefit of fewer crashes altogether.

Voluntary safety helmet use by those accident-involved motorcycle riders was lowest for untrained, uneducated, young motorcycle riders on hot days and short trips.

For whom do we fear most? How about the not-very-worldly 18-year-old who's (halfheartedly) spending his first summer of freedom in summer school and riding his cool new sport bike (Mom and Dad helped finance it) up to the lake to attract young females in bikinis? The young, being invincible *and* good looking, don't use helmets for obvious reasons, and you can't wear leather to the beach. Hot weather and short trips, I think, are still the most common reasons why people who would normally wear protective gear choose not

to wear it.

I'll bet young, uneducated, and untrained people take unnecessary risks in almost every physical activity. Sometimes, we need to learn the hard way. I know I did. As far as hot days and short trips, it's very simple: If it's too hot to wear the gear, it's too hot to ride the bike. If it's too short a trip to wear the gear, it's too close to ride the bike. That's what cars are for—hot days and short trips.

The most deadly injuries to the accident victims were injuries to the chest and head.

Hmmm . . . Your heart and lungs are located in your chest. Your brain is located in your head. You don't need a medical degree to figure out the repercussions. However, it's good to note that, when in a crash, it is most important to protect your head and chest. Are there ways to protect these areas in addition to wearing good protective gear?

The use of the safety helmet is the single critical factor in the prevention or reduction of head injury; the safety helmet, which complies with FMVSS 218, is a significantly effective injury countermeasure.

Oh, boy . . . now we're into it. Helmets help prevent injuries. Well, duh. FMVSS 218 is the DOT helmet standard. (You know, the little stickers they sell at swap meets so you can turn that plastic salad bowl into a "legal" helmet.) I'm a big helmet-use supporter and hate to see people riding without them, especially those who believe that they will be more seriously injured if they crash while wearing one. Some reasonable (and educated) people still honestly believe that helmets cause neck injuries. The grim reality is that *crashing* causes the neck injuries, and the helmet likely even reduces the severity of *those*. If you hit your head hard enough to break your neck, the helmet certainly isn't going to make it any worse.

I will concede the possibility that a helmet, not a crash (well, it's *still* the crash), can actually cause a neck injury. A crash in which a motorcyclist is rear-ended at *just* the right speed, the speed at which he or she can remain upright and in control of the bike but receives a whiplash type of injury is the one possible example I can imagine. The speed would have to be just enough for the weight of the helmet to cause an injury, but not enough for the impact to have caused an injury no matter what. I doubt that it's ever even happened.

While I'm not a proponent of helmet *laws*, and hate to see federal mandates on safety issues, I'm certainly a strong believer in wearing helmets, but there are plenty of people who don't wear helmets for whatever reason.

Safety helmet use caused no attenuation of critical traffic sounds, no limitation of precrash visual field, and no fatigue or loss of attention; no element of accident causation was related to helmet use. FMVSS 218 provides a high level of protection in traffic accidents, and needs modification only to increase coverage at the back of the head and demonstrate impact protection of the front of full facial coverage helmets, and ensure all adult sizes for traffic use are covered by the standard.

Hurt, in this statement, claims that neither visual field nor important traffic noises are diminished to a point where they contributed to a crash. The DOT standard requires a 210-degree field of peripheral vision, while humans, at best, have about 180 degrees of peripheral vision. Also, while sound is certainly attenuated by a three-quarter or full-face helmet, including wind and exhaust noise, it is important to note that *all* sounds are reduced by the same amount. That horn honking will be just as audible in relation to the wind noise inside the helmet as it would outside. It's just that the wind noise won't be damaging your eardrums in the meantime. I hate to beat a dead horse, and I have a sneaking suspicion that I'm preaching to the choir here, so I'll let it go at that.

Helmeted riders and passengers showed significantly lower head and neck injury for all types of injury, at all levels of injury severity.

Well, what did you expect?

The increased coverage of the full facial coverage helmet increases protection and significantly reduces face injuries.

For those people who are comfortable wearing a full-face helmet, the reduction of injuries to the facial area is great. I had a spill while riding a demonstration in an MSF course that I was teaching a few years ago. In addition to the minor injuries I

Do helmets cause neck injuries? No. Crashing does. Then why do neck injuries go up in states that enact mandatory helmet laws? Because corpses don't complain about sore necks.

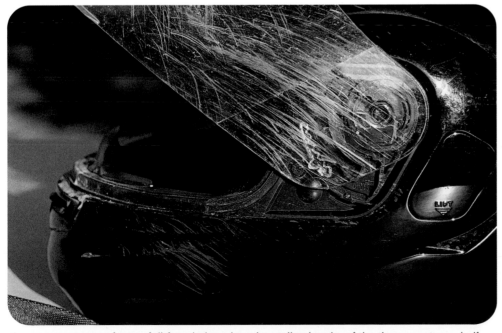

As you move away from a full-face helmet into the stylized realm of the three-quarter or half helmet, your risk of injury goes up—sure, you're protecting your skull, but what about the other, pointier, softer parts? Protecting yourself against a possibly fatal head injury is wise. Also protecting yourself against a debilitating face injury, in addition to wind, rain, bugs, sand, debris, and other airborne detritus is truly risk-averse. Imagine the look on this rider's face had she been wearing a three-quarter helmet with a microphone. The chin bar probably didn't save her life, but it sure saved her good looks.

Minnesota has some 330,000 licensed riders and 200,000 bikes. But only 150,000 bikes are currently registered. So who owns them? License data shows that women comprise 8.5 percent of all licensed riders. But registration data says they comprise 10.5 percent of bike owners. (A recent survey suggests that number is nearly 15 percent.) So which is it? We have 150,000 bikes, but the average ownership is 1.8 bikes per owner. So how many riders do we really have?

Harry Hurt found that riders don't subject themselves to greater risk of neck injury by wearing a helmet. Helmeted riders had fewer neck injuries than unhelmeted riders in the study. Only four minor injuries were attributable to helmet use, and in each case the helmet prevented possible critical or fatal head injury. That's four injuries out of approximately 3,600.

sustained, a large chip was taken out of the chin bar of my helmet. I shudder to think of what could have happened had I been wearing a three-quarter helmet or half shell. One of the comment cards I received after the class read as follows:

Q. "What was the most useful thing about this class?"

A. "The demonstration where I learned I needed a better helmet."

There is not liability for neck injury by wearing a safety helmet; helmeted riders had fewer neck injuries than unhelmeted riders did. Only four minor injuries were attributable to helmet use, and in each case the helmet prevented possible critical or fatal head injury.

"Helmets cause injuries" is one of the many arguments from the anti-helmet crowd. In Hurt's study, as indicated, there were only four injuries related to the helmet—four out of more than 3,600 crashes. Those injuries involved a person wearing the wrong sized helmet and the helmet either sliding forward and crunching his glasses onto his nose, or sliding backward and scraping the skin of the neck. Either way, it's worth checking the opposing view, but the truth is that you're

better off with a helmet on your head—*if living to tell about it is your goal.*

Sixty percent of the motorcyclists were not wearing safety helmets at the time of the accident. Of this group, 26 percent said they did not wear helmets because they were uncomfortable and inconvenient, and 53 percent simply had no expectation of accident involvement.

If those 53 percent had been told before getting on their bike that day that they would be in an accident, would it have made a difference? Would they have donned a helmet? Would they have ridden any differently? Would they have ridden at all? Expecting that every time you ride your trip will end in a reverberating crash and shower of sparks and broken plastic should keep you in the risk-averse frame of mind.

Hurt's Conclusions

Valid motorcycle exposure data can be obtained only from collection at the traffic site. Motor vehicle or driver license data presents information, which is completely unrelated to actual use.

In my own state we know that a rider has a one in 100 chance of a crash, men crash more than women, young people crash more than old people, and that alcohol is involved in about half the fatalities. But what do we really know about why riders crash?

Hurt is correct in that the only way to derive solid conclusions about motorcycle crashes is to be there when they happen, record as much data as possible, and follow up to get the complete story. Modern basic motor vehicle demographic data is helpful, but not sufficient. It's great to know how many riders died, how many were injured, what the age ranges were, and how many of them were actually licensed, but without being able to cross reference these numbers we can't draw more than very basic conclusions. A lot is left to intuition and anecdote. A proposal for another comprehensive motorcycle crash study is before the national legislature, and hopefully we'll see some significant research in the next decade. We need it.

Fewer than 10 percent of the motorcycle riders involved in these accidents had insurance of any kind to provide medical care or replace property.

Again, this is most likely a throwback to the late 1970s and early 1980s when motorcycle transport was a cheap way of getting to work or school ("cheap" being the operative word.) With motorcycles being more expensive and insurance coverage required by law in most areas, this is less of a concern, as people are protecting their investments with insurance.

It's interesting to note, however, that some states offer riders the choice of helmet use if they hold a minimum of $10,000 in medical insurance. I have a very difficult time believing ten grand is going to make much of a difference when it comes to hospital bills for an unhelmeted rider. I think somebody just traded away their freedoms for a red herring.

If you'd like to get a copy of the entire Hurt Study, the order information is:

Motorcycle Accident Cause Factors and Identification of Countermeasures, Volume 1: Technical Report, Hurt, H. H., Ouellet, J. V., and Thom, D. R., Traffic Safety Center, University of Southern California, Los Angeles, California 90007, Contract No. DOT HS-5-01160, January 1981 (Final Report).

This document is available through the National Technical Information Service, Springfield, Virginia 22161.

Before You Hit the Road
- Understand that a rider's biggest risk is usually himself or herself.
- Take a very close look at your reasons for riding.
- Find yourself in the Hurt Study and adapt your strategy to it.
- Find others in the Hurt Study and teach them.
- Separate drinking and riding. Mercilessly mock those who don't.
- Wear the gear, but fight the laws that try to require it.

In 2003, legislators began looking at funding another in-depth motorcycle crash study. Contact them and let 'em know what a good idea you think that is.

c h a p t e r   3

RISK

This book is all about risk.

Every thing we do has some degree of risk, no matter what. There is no situation imaginable in which a person faces absolutely no risk. Look at it this way: Reading this book on your couch is risky—not very risky, but some risk exists, nonetheless. Let's say on a scale of 1 to 10, reading this book has a level of, oh, about 1 (I'll round up). It's unlikely, but anything could happen. You could get a paper cut and bleed to death. You could have a heart attack. You could fall asleep and your house could catch fire. A meteorite could come crashing through the roof. Your neighbor's lawnmower could throw a blade and decapitate you where you sit. The universe could suddenly collapse back upon itself. None of these things are very likely to happen, but the risk still exists. Risk Level: 1.

Usually without even thinking about it, the average human weighs the risks and decides whether or not they're worth it. The chances of grievous injury in the case of reading a book on the couch are too small to dissuade you and relate only indirectly to reading this book, so you take the risk. It would be fair to call it a calculated risk.

The risks associated with reading this book don't necessarily come from reading, but the combination of who you are, what you're doing, and the environment in which you're

Reading in your backyard has a certain level of risk based on three factors: who you are, what you're doing, and where you are doing it. Reading on an airplane probably has the same level of risk (1) as reading on the couch, but based on different factors. Reading while driving a car has different risk factors too, but that particular combination shoots the risk factor way up to, say, 10.

doing it. Reading in your house has a certain level of risk based on these three factors. Reading on an airplane probably has the same level of risk (1) but based on different factors. Reading while driving a car has different risk factors too, but that particular combination shoots the risk factor way up to, say, 10.

Riding a motorcycle terrifies me. Driving in general terrifies me. There are millions of other drivers out there, and any one of them could have your number. Every one of them, if the timing is right, does have your number. Leave your house five seconds earlier or five seconds later, you face an entirely different scenario. People make mistakes all the time. I make mistakes all the time. When a motorcycle rider and the driver of a car each make a mistake at the exact same time and in the exact same place, the results can be especially deadly. The luck of timing has everything to do with whether you make it home or not. Can you affect your timing? Yes. Can you foresee what difference five seconds will make? Sometimes.

As someone with a paralyzing fear of pain and injury, I devote enormous quantities of energy to analyzing my risks and finding ways to reduce them. Put it this way: If you have to walk a tightrope on a sunny day, and you can choose to do it either with or without a baseball cap, which way is less risky? That's what I'm talking about.

By analyzing yourself, your bike, and your environment, you can compare factors and situations and find ways to tweak your riding style to reduce the likelihood that you'll suffer accident or injury.

I will try to do so in relative terms ("This is more or less risky than that") and absolute terms ("This has a risk level of such and such"). My rating system is completely arbitrary, totally make-believe, and is meant to illustrate risk, not measure it. I will begin with these reference points:

Risk Level 1: Resting state, lowest possible risk. You can breathe easy. A freak accident is the only thing that stands between you and a long life. This state is impossible to achieve on a moving motorcycle. Example: a hammock hung over a pile of fluffy pillows stacked on top of one of those big mattresses the stunt guys use when they jump off of buildings.

Risk Level 2: Everyday risk. Like driving a car, crossing the street, or golfing. On a motorcycle, this level is only possible with a firm grasp of the three degrees of separation *and* using them in a controlled environment. Example: throwing red paint on a 50-year-old woman wearing a fur coat.

Risk Level 3: Controlled risk. Like scuba diving, skiing, or engaging in professional sports. You can achieve this level riding a motorcycle on the street with the three degrees of separation and a lot of luck. Examples: driving a car without wearing a seatbelt, eating improperly prepared food.

Risk Level 4: Annoying risk. This is the equivalent of riding a bicycle on the street with a flagrant disregard for traffic laws or recklessly driving in a car. Examples: riding a motorcycle without protective gear, smoking.

Risk Level 5: Foolish risk. This is no safer than unprotected casual sex. Examples: riding without protective gear or rider training, combining alcohol with any sort of power tools.

Risk Level 6: Stupid risk. Drinking and driving comes to mind, as does riding without gear, motorcycle skills, or a strategy. Examples: mountain climbing, extramarital affairs.

Risk Level 7: Social-pariah risk. Okay, you've reached the level of stupidity reserved for those who are driving while intoxicated. Equate this level with reckless riding using the three degrees of separation or learning how to ride a motorcycle for the first time on public streets. Examples: unsanctioned bungee jumping, sanctioned bungee jumping.

Risk Level 8: Martyr-envy risk. Here, you'd be doing 220-volt electrical work without switching off the power, or reading and driving. It's also equivalent to pointing a fake gun at a peace officer or recklessly riding *without* using the three degrees of separation. Examples: impaired riding, throwing red paint on a bunch of Hell's Angels wearing patches. In front of their old ladies.

Three primary factors contribute to risk: who you are, what you are doing, and where you're doing it. All the things that put you at risk on your motorcycle fall into one of these three categories.

Taking the ideas presented here and analyzing for yourself the risk factors involved in motorcycling will give you a clearer view of which ones you're willing to accept, which ones you're not, and which ones you can do something about.

Risk Level	Name	Example 1	Example 2	Motorcycling Equivalent
1	Resting	Reading on the Couch	Sleeping on an air mattress in a locked Brick House.	Not Possible
2	Everyday	Golfing	Throwing Paint at Old Ladies	Three Degrees in a Controlled Environment
3	Controlled	Skiing	Undercooked Meat	Three Degrees on the Street
4	Annoying	Reckless Driving	Smoking	Riding without Protective Gear
5	Foolish	Unprotected Sex	Beer and Power Tools	Riding without Protective Gear or Training
6	Stupid	Mountain Climbing	Extramarital Affairs	Riding without Gear, Training or Stratedgy
7	Social-Pariah	Driving Intoxicated	Bungee Jumping	Reckless Riding
8	Martyr-Envy	Reading and Driving	Throwing Paint at Bikers	Impaired Riding
9	Suicidal	Riding Intoxicated	Heroin	Riding Drunk
10	Certain Death	Chuteless Parachuting	"Hasta-la-Vista, Baby"	Riding Drunk and Recklessly

Old Veemax Vince in Chapter I would slide right purty into Risk Level 6. Vince wasn't necessarily stupid, but he was taking a stupid risk. Several of them, actually.

A crash is what happens when two or more risk factors come together in the same place at the same time. A blown tire is a risk factor but really not so dangerous in and of itself. Combine it with an off-camber curve, now you have two factors working in cooperation to separate you from your bike and both of you from the road. Add in a third factor, like poor skills or heavy traffic, and the risk multiplies.

Risk Level 9: Suicidal risk. People you don't know are praying for your soul. You run red lights. You race trains. You try to outdo that Crocodile-Hunter guy. You ride while intoxicated. Examples: injecting heroin, unprotected, anonymous sex in a Kenyan bathhouse.

Risk Level 10: Certain-death risk. You can measure your life expectancy in minutes. Examples: jumping from an airplane without a chute; riding a motorcycle at 10 over the limit in suburban rush hour traffic at twilight while intoxicated; being a bad guy in a Schwarzenegger movie.

Riding a motorcycle means accepting a higher level of risk than most people are willing to accept. Whether you know what the risks are or you don't, whether you take steps to manage them or you don't, whether you realize you are entering into a compromise with the gods of chance or not, by choosing to ride a motorcycle you are accepting an elevated level of risk.

There's no way around it. You are choosing to make a compromise between risks and rewards. The risks, of course, are death, injury, pain, property damage, and the psychological damage from having your friends and family laugh and point when you are trying to show off in the front yard and instead put your bike into the neighbor's rosebushes. The rewards, of course, are fun, freedom, travel, transportation, economy, and the social stigma that goes along with being "the biker guy" in the neighborhood or "that racer dude" who parks on the sidewalk at work.

Crashes absolutely don't happen because of one single risk factor. A crash is what happens when one or more risk factors come together in the same place at the same time. A blown tire is a risk factor, but is really not so dangerous in and of itself. If the tire blows while you're motionless in your driveway, the only real risk is giving the cat a heart attack. But combine a blown tire with an off-camber curve, now you have two factors working in cooperation to separate you from your bike and both of you from the road. Now you've got a problem. You've added another risk factor and doubled—or, rather, multiplied—your overall risk. Add in a third factor, like poor riding skills or heavy traffic, and the risk multiplies again.

But pulling even one minor risk factor out of the mix lowers the chance of a mishap dramatically. When one plus one equals two, one factor plus another factor equals two factors, which is the minimum you need to crash—assume, at that point, that your risk doubles. Riding inevitably allows the number of risk factors to pile up, one on top of the other, and risk grows exponentially. But paying close attention and methodically removing risk factors as they become evident lowers the risk dramatically. By understanding the level of risk each factor presents and eliminating or reducing them one at a time, a rider can gradually reduce the inevitable confluence of Bad Things.

Some riders' perceptions of the risks they face are not so acute.

Any time the number or risk factors goes over one, you're at risk. Whenever you add another factor to the mix, you're going to have a more difficult time dealing with surprises. When one plus zero equals one, you're still in safe mode. One factor generally cannot hurt you, except in the case of what we professionals call an "act of God."

But as shown in the Risk Level table, the risk of riding a motorcycle isn't always the same. It changes from day to day and from minute to minute when it comes to things like mobile offices, 40 mile-per-hour makeup artists, Chez Geo's fast-food catch of the day, and the inevitable clunker spewing various fluids to port, starboard, and dead center. For a talented rider, these are the biggest hazards you'll face—the risks forced upon you by other people. The reason they're the biggest hazards is that you can do so very little to control them.

We're going to ignore the possibility of rider error for the rest of this book and concentrate on things like road-bound realtors, teen CD hunters, and the inevitable disaster vehicle leaving a trail of fluids like a submissive puppy. These are the biggest hazards you face—those forced upon you, over which you have no control.

Or do you?

What you can control is the level of risk at which you place yourself. Again, look back to the Risk Level table. For some people, Risk Level 10 is an acceptable compromise. The rewards they get outweigh the almost certain possibility that the activities will end badly. But for most of us, we'd choose not to take ourselves into the realm of certain death. For what we get out of it, the rush of falling from an airplane, the fun of drinking with your buddies after work and then blasting home on your bike, the notion that you could put one over on the old Terminator just isn't worth it. So we adjust our actions to take us to a lower level of risk—one in which the rewards are worth the perceived risk we choose to face.

The further you remove yourself from Risk Level 1, the more you put your life in danger. How much danger depends on how far from the resting rate you choose to go. There you are, at the resting rate, lying in your hammock in the shade over all the fluffy pillows, when you decide you need a glass of lemonade. The thought of the refreshing soft drink quenching your thirst carries more weight than the thought of what might happen if you fell down the steps going

Risk avoidance also means understanding that risk factors need to pile up in order to cause a crash. By understanding the level of risk each factor presents, and eliminating or reducing them one at a time, a rider can gradually reduce the inevitable convergence of Bad Things.

A jump from resting rate to stupid risk shouldn't be done lightly. Understanding that you're making the jump at all is the first and most critical step. Understanding why *you're suddenly going from Level 1 to Level 6 is next. What factors are involved? Doing something to lessen or eliminate the risk factors that take you from Level 1 to Level 6 is the goal.*

Every increase in speed starts you up the chain of risk.

to the refrigerator. A tumble into the basement is not very likely, while the likelihood of a cold bottle of beer or tumbler of lemonade soothing your throat is highly likely. So you make the choice, accept the compromise, take your risks and earn your rewards. Mmmm . . . lemonade.

Yet another way to estimate relative risk is to understand how something as simple as speed affects it. In the previous example, we started with a blown tire. One risk factor, not a big deal. We then added an off-camber corner. That's two risk factors, and two that can work together to unseat you. However, a blown tire and an off-camber curve at zero miles per hour is almost no risk, right? But who wants to sit at home all day when there's a motorcycle to be ridden? So you start taking chances, and any movement away from the hammock and the fluffy pillows is a compromise of your

safety. Blowing a tire in an off-camber curve at 30 miles per hour is very different from blowing one at zero, as is one at 60 miles per hour. Every increase in speed starts you up the chain of risk.

Let's look at it from another, more familiar, perspective. Here I am, at my resting rate, banging away at the computer keyboard with a photo of my snarling editor tacked to the dartboard, grinning down at me. I'm not facing too much risk right now. But I gaze out the window, notice that the sun has come out, and the recently rain-washed streets are drying up nicely, and the temperature is again rising. Note to self: You've been working too hard. Maybe it's time to go for a motorcycle ride?

What am I giving up? I'm giving up Level 1 to jump immediately to Level 6, the basic motorcycling level of risk. I'm giving up the safety and surety of being chained to my desk, and instead choosing to replace it with the rewards of the summer wind, the fresh, clean air, the pull of the engine and the howl of the exhaust pipe, the grip of gravity as I flick my bike into a nicely banked corner, the freedom and fun and soul-soothing effect that riding has on me. For most people, this is a good tradeoff.

But not me. Any leap from Level 1 straight to Level 6 gives me dizzy goosebumps. The little alarm goes off in my head. I've got a family to think about. I've got people who depend on me. What would my editor do if I never finished the book? I already spent the advance on new tires and a tank bag. I simply can't give up the resting-rate risk level where I'm sure of a glorious old age and trade it for the self-indulgent rewards of an unstrategized, untrained, unadorned ride on the motorcycle, no matter how much fun that might be.

It's just a little too self-absorbed for my risk-averse sensibilities.

Hmmm. I'd really like to take a break and go for a ride, though. Is there any way I can do it without accepting Risk Level 6? Maybe.

I do have some good riding gear in the closet. The helmet's almost new, the gloves are worn and comfortable, the suit sticks out like a sore thumb, armor, padding, and pockets, the boots are looking good still. That'd take me down to Level 5.

I did take that motorcycle class. I learned all about how to spot hazards. I learned how to brake and swerve and steer in an emergency. My good skills could take me down to Level 4. Hmmm . . . a ride is looking more and more likely. And, I do have a pretty good riding strategy that takes the surprises out of most days. I like to practice and refine it as I go, because there's always more to learn. All right, I've got the three degrees of separation and I could use them—that'd take me down to Level 3. Can I accept that level of risk? Now it's starting to look a little better. But is there any way I can get down to Level 2?

I'd really like to get down to Level 2. While it's not as surefire safe as 1, it's as safe as I can get on a moving motorcycle. The street is unfortunately just too unpredictable and carries too many variables. I can't control luck, and trailering the bike

to the racetrack probably isn't possible or realistic when I know I have to be back here in a few hours anyway. But there's got to be a way to get to Level 2 without a controlled environment. Could there be?

Maybe. Read on.

As I mentioned above, now that we've made it all the way down to risk Level 3, we are more or less tossing out the concept of rider error for the rest of the book. This is not to say that rider error doesn't exist, we're just going to ignore it because that's not what this book is really about. The concepts that follow will almost entirely disregard any fault on the part of the rider. If you're reading this book, you probably have your skills and brain up to par, and the biggest risks you face are from the Other Guy, anyway. We're going to concentrate on him. Her. *Them.*

Before You Hit the Road

- The further you are from zero miles per hour, the higher you are on the scale of risk.
- You have complete control over 90 percent of the risks you face.
- It takes at least two risk factors to cause a crash.

I'd really like to get away from this desk and take a motorcycle ride, but that forces me straight from Level 1 to Level 6, and I'm not willing to accept that risk. However, I do wear protective gear—that takes me to Level 5. And I did take the safety class and learned how to do those cool tricks. Now I'm at 4. I play my riding strategy like a game, so I'm already down to 3. But is there a way to achieve Level 2?

THE SAFEST DISTANCE BETWEEN TWO POINTS

There are about a million different ways to get from any Point A to any Point B.

If two different routes will get you to the same destination, which one do you take? Let's pretend you have decided to ride your bike to work every day. You have a choice: You can either take the freeway (along with everybody else in the known universe) or the side roads. The freeway is three lanes wide, the traffic moves at about 70, and you can get to work in half the time it takes on the side roads. On the other hand, the side roads are one or two lanes wide, move at about 30 or 40, see little traffic, and get you to work in double the time the freeway takes. Let's pretend it's a 20-minute difference. Forty minutes a day. If time is of the essence, the choice is obvious. But for argument's sake, what are the other considerations?

Speed

What is it about freeways and rural highways that make fatal crashes more likely? What is it about city streets and populated areas that make injuries and property damage the more common results of a crash?

Your risks change as your speed changes. The consequences of a mistake at 30 miles per hour are likely to be less dramatic than the consequences at 60 miles per hour. Or put another

There is something about freeways (and rural highways) that makes fatal crashes more likely than on urban and suburban streets. There's also something about city streets and populated areas that makes injury and property damage crashes more common. Remember, your risks change with changes in the flow of traffic. The results of a mishap at 30 miles per hour in town are far less likely to be as horrific as the results of the same mistake at 60 on the highway. If you knew you were going to crash, at which speed would you rather do it?

Odds are this guy's not going to have all his stuff when he gets to his new house. Now you know where those roadside couches and chairs come from.

way, if you knew you were going to crash, at which speed would you rather do it?

You'll need quite a bit more time and space to react at 60 than at 30. How far ahead do you need to scan? A 12-second visual lead translates into 1/5 of a mile at 60 miles per hour. But that makes it 1/10 of a mile at 30 miles per hour, right? Look at it this way: Does a deer standing at the side of the road a quarter-mile away pose more risk to the rider at 30 miles per hour or the rider at 60 miles per hour?

How many more feet does it take to stop a bike at 60 miles per hour than at 30 miles per hour? How many feet will the motorcycle travel between when you notice a hazard and when you begin braking—your reaction time? Average reaction time is about 0.5 seconds, or 22 feet at 30 miles per hour and 44 feet at 60. Will those feet make a critical difference? Remember, as speed increases, braking distance increases—geometrically. If it takes 43 feet to stop your bike at 30 miles per hour, it'll take you 172 feet to stop your bike at 60. And that doesn't include reaction time. So, all other things being equal, less speed equals less risk.

If you had to swerve quickly to avoid a hazard, at which speed would you prefer to do it, 30 miles per hour or 60 miles per hour? Swerving at high speeds requires a great deal more traction and precision than swerving at lower speeds.

At lower speeds, the added amount of time and space you have to work with—if your scanning is good and decision making prompt—will help allow you to make multiple maneuvers when you need to.

Predictability

Your hazards on the freeway are entirely different from your hazards on the side roads.

Are you more likely or less likely to be surprised on the freeway? There's usually a physical barrier in the middle, so hazards crossing over from the other side are not too common. The interchanges are fewer, with access controlled. They're consistently marked, and have acceleration and deceleration lanes. There are rarely any reasons to stop. You know that the left lane is for passing and for people in a really big hurry. You know the right lane is for out-of-town blue haireds and merging. In metropolitan areas, there are usually fences to keep the area animal- and pedestrian-free. But you do know to expect debris in the road. Tire carcasses, dry wall, furniture, car bumpers—these things fly off vehicles all the time. Speed has that effect on unsecured loads. The wind can whip garbage around. Because of speed and proximity to other vehicles, most times you aren't aware of these things until you're already on top of them. So overall, freeways equal more predictability equals less risk.

In town, you don't have the luxury of all this predictability. You've got side streets coming in from all different angles. You've got stoplights and stop signs, which are highly visible, but sometimes viewed by the locals as optional. You've got yield signs that are even easier to ignore. The speed limit varies. The width of the road varies. Lanes end, turn, and merge. Some traffic moves at the speed limit, some traffic moves very slowly, some traffic doesn't realize it's no longer on the freeway.

All else being equal:

*Freeways
=
higher speed
=
higher risk.*

*Side streets
=
lower speed
=
lower risk.*

*Once again,
all else being equal:*

*Freeways
=
more predictable
=
less risk.*

*Sides streets
=
less predictable
=
more risk.*

On the freeway, the difference between the slowest vehicle and the fastest vehicle is relatively small—for example, 40 in the right lane and 75 in the left—a difference of about 60 percent. (I arrive at this number by dividing the difference in speed by the average speed, on the freeway 35/57.5 = 0.60 and in town 40/20 = 2. These numbers are arbitrary, but they serve the point. See the end of this chapter for further simplification and analysis.) This is still enough of a difference to cause amazing problems. The impossibly slow parades of harried commuters on ramps, combined with the clustered conga line in the right lane, do much to increase everyone's risk.

Statistically, you're less likely to die but more likely to be involved in a crash on slower roads. Conversely, you're more likely to die but less likely to be involved in a crash on faster roads. In which circumstances are you more willing to take the risk? Which are your better-honed skills, perception and attention or swerving and braking?

You've got gas stations, fast food, and convenience stores. You've got bars and you've got schools. You've got painted lines, railroad tracks, and parked cars. You've got people with pets, joggers, bicyclists, in-line skaters, and little kids chasing balls or pulling kites. There's a lot more to pay attention to, and be distracted by, on the side streets. There are many more places for hazards to hide. So, all else being equal, side streets equal less predictability equals more risk.

Speed and Predictability

The relationships between speed and risk and between predictability and risk make the choice between the fast road and the slow road kind of a wash. What you give up in one area, you gain back in the other. Statistically, you're less likely to die but more likely to be involved in a crash on the slower roads. Conversely, you're more likely to die but less likely to be involved in a crash on the faster roads. In which circumstances are you more willing to take the risk? How do you feel about minor mishaps and

injuries? How much do you fear dying? Which type of riding do you prefer? Is your concentration and ability to focus more suited to higher or lower speeds, and to more or fewer vehicles on the road? Are your crash avoidance skills like swerving and braking your strong suit, or do your observational skills and ability to avoid hazards keep you safe?

Relative Speed

Why is it that more crashes happen on the side streets and back roads than on the freeways? The variety of speeds on the same roadway is one way to explain it.

On the freeway, the difference between the slowest vehicle and the fastest vehicle is relatively small—for example, 40 miles per hour in the right lane and 75 miles per hour in the left—a difference of about 60 percent. Another example is a slow parade of vehicles trying to negotiate a ramp at 30 while simultaneously trying to merge with another conga line of vehicles going 60. The risks on the freeway in steady traffic go way up in merging areas, and when someone's traveling dramatically slower than everyone else.

Around town, the difference between the slowest vehicle and the fastest is far greater. Take as an example a landscaping truck pulling out into traffic from a dead stop while you're cruising along at the posted 40—the speed differential is 200 percent. Which is more predictable? Freeways equal less relative speed diff ulling out into traffic from a dead stop while you're cruising along at the posted 40 creates a speed differential of 200 percent.

Truly, It's All about Speed

The biggest factor (three degrees of separation aside) that affects your risk is speed. The odds are that a mishap at a slower speed will have fewer or less dramatic consequences than one at a higher speed. This means that your first consideration, under any circumstances, when confronting any hazard, real or imagined, should be to adjust your speed to minimize your risk. Fortunately, this is one factor over which you have complete control. Go ahead and compare which is preferable:

• Slower speeds reduce the rate at which hazards approach.

• Higher speeds increase the rate at which hazards approach.

• Slower speeds reduce the amount of traction you need to perform evasive maneuvers.

• Higher speeds increase the amount of traction you need to perform evasive maneuvers.

• Slower speeds reduce the severity of a crash by reducing the impact forces.

• Higher speeds increase the severity of a crash by increasing the impact forces.

Braking hard is the simplest way to reduce your risk in a hurry. Not only do you buy yourself time and space to make your next decision, you lessen the severity and extent of injuries if you do end up crashing.

Road Surfaces

When choosing between the slow route and the fast route, which one has better pavement? Which has less of the traditional oil slick down the center? Where do farmers, logging trucks, or the aftermath of torrential rains affect available traction? On which surface are you more likely to find potholes? Diesel spills? Which route will be easier to negotiate in the rain? Which turns are banked properly, and which are off-camber? Does the camber of the road help or hinder your control? How does the surface change when it rains? What about when it's cold? Better surface equals fewer traction hazards equals less risk.

Traffic

Where do you encounter more traffic—the freeway, or the side roads? Does the time of day you travel make a difference? First-shift workers (7 a.m. until 3 p.m.) probably have to deal with the brunt of rush-hour congestion, while second- and third-shift workers (3 to 11 p.m. and 11 to 7, respectively) only have to deal with half of it. When traveling, try to plan riding through populated areas during times when traffic is light, or at least when traffic is most predictable.

If you commute, experiment with leaving a few minutes earlier or a few minutes later than you need to. I've noticed that the traffic I deal with at 7:15 a.m. is quite a bit different from that at 6:45. The same thing goes in the afternoon. The traffic at 3:45 p.m. is quite a bit different from that at 4:15. Consider adjusting your work schedule to decrease your risk and make the trip more enjoyable. Thus, less traffic equals fewer hazards equals less risk.

Daylight

Do you ride during the day or at night? Do you ride east in the morning and west in the evening, or vice-versa? Or neither? Do you live in an area where all sorts of critters come out at night?

In higher-latitude areas like the United States, especially the northern half, dawn and dusk last a long time—that's a longer period of time for the sun to be glaring into your eyes, just above the horizon. This might be a good time to take a break. But in high-latitude areas, the sun's arc changes constantly, and where the sun can cause problems on a certain road at a certain time, a half-hour later or earlier can make all the difference in the world. Two weeks earlier or two weeks later can also make all the difference in the world.

Consider adjusting your travel plans or work hours to allow you—and others—

With all other variables being equal, we know: Lower speed equals less risk. More predictability equals less risk. Less relative speed difference equals less risk. Better surface equals less risk Less traffic equals less risk. Good daylight equals less risk.

This bike has an intended purpose, and that purpose sure isn't commuting in city traffic.

If you use your bike to get back and forth to work, experiment with your travel times—try leaving a little earlier or a little later. I've noticed that the traffic I deal with at 7:15 a.m. is quite a bit different from that at 7:45. The same thing goes in the afternoon. The traffic at 4:15 p.m. is quite a bit different from that at 4:45. Consider adjusting your work schedule to decrease your risk and increase your smiles-per-mile.

plenty of daylight to observe and blend smoothly with the flow of traffic. If you must travel during sunset and twilight, try to choose a route that doesn't put you or the other road users at a disadvantage. Or at least, choose a route that doesn't compromise *your* vision (see Chapter 6). So, good daylight equals better vision equals less risk.

Comfort level

Upon which roads are you most comfortable? Upon which roads are you too confident?

If you're used to riding on open roads at high speeds, city streets may cause you undue anxiety. If you are most familiar with city streets, suburban four-laners might terrify you. If you are accustomed to the suburbs, the entire outside world probably unnerves you. Your comfort and confidence in your ability and control of the world around you are important considerations. Sometimes it's best to stick with what you know. Which type of traffic is more predictable to you? When other, uncontrollable factors move in to increase your risk, it's best to stick with a route you know, or the type of riding with which you're most familiar.

However, this blade has a double edge. Being overly familiar with a route or a type of road can make you overconfident, lazy, or even apathetic toward surprises. To keep my mental skills sharp and that pang of

fear always at hand, I mix up my routes from time to time to give the old brain a wake-up call. I started on city streets and was uncomfortable at any speed over about 40. Eventually, by taking different routes to work and for fun, I became familiar enough with the variety of roads in my area that I felt competent with all of them, but I rode none of them often enough to get overconfident with any of them.

That said, when you're at risk for some other reason—poor surface, heavy traffic, poor lighting, fatigue, stress, emotion—it may be smartest to stick with the route you know best.

Familiarity

Have you gotten to know every curve, crest, and bump on your route? Could you do it in your sleep? (Would you want to?) Have you traversed the same roads for years without any close calls? Familiarity reduces the amount of new information your brain needs to process on a ride. But monotony can make you complacent and inattentive— a very dangerous state of mind on two wheels. Ask yourself, are you better off being relaxed or nervous when you ride? Choose the road or the route upon which you'll be *attentive* first, *familiar* second.

Mileage/Wear and Tear

What sort of riding and speeds are better for your particular bike? A larger road bike with a big engine may like the freeway better, whereas a smaller dual-sport or sport bike may be more at home in the city and at slower speeds. A lightweight bike may handle multiple stops and starts better than a heavier one. Higher speeds will wear out your tires faster. Is your trip long enough to get your bike up to operating temperature? What about your tires?

There are so many ways to skin the commuting cat. Sure, this way may take longer, but the risks are so much lower and you have the added benefits of looking forward to going to work and always coming home with a smile on your face.

Convenience

Sure, the freeway is faster, but is it always faster? When the weather is bad, or there's a crash, do you spend the same amount of time on the freeway? On the other hand, the side roads always move slower, but the amount of time you spend on them won't change much. The variations in travel time with regard to traffic conditions can be likened to the relative difference in speed. A 20-minute freeway trip with a crash can turn into 40 or 60 minutes (200–300 percent increase), depending on where you live and the road design. A crash on the side streets could turn a 40-minute ride into a 50- or 60-minute ride (25 percent increase). How common are variations in travel time?

Inner Peace

Do you get as much time in the saddle as you'd like?

When deciding which way to take, think also of the fringe benefits. If you're going to spend extra time on the road, it should be for fun, not for struggling to get home in one piece. If you took the long way, would it cost you time that you'd rather spend elsewhere? Or is the trip you make the only opportunity you'll get to spend riding that day? Would you prefer to stretch it out and enjoy it, as long as you're making the trip anyway?

During my first year as a rider, I lived in downtown Chicago and worked in a northern suburb. I'd chosen not to own a car, and rode my bike every day it was above freezing—it was either that or the city bus. The worst day riding was always better than the best day on the bus.

I had two choices: 20 minutes on the Edens Expressway, a hair-raising 75-miles-per-hour ride, or 40 minutes on winding, residential Sheridan Road at a sedate 30. The freeway was noisy, dirty, and terrifying. I made one turn to get on the freeway, and one to get off. Otherwise, the route was a straight, uninspiring line. Sheridan Road, however, was quiet, calm, and relaxing. It began at the tip of the city, and twisted and turned along the lakeshore with sand, wind, trees, mansions, gates, and garden gnomes. It always took the same amount of time. It meandered north along Lake Michigan, through beautiful, silent neighborhoods, along perfectly manicured parks, and through the Northwestern University campus. The sun would rise on my right on my way to work; the light would reflect off the waves and through the trees. The cool lake breeze always felt great in the summertime.

The ride was so consistently pleasant that I was invariably smiling when I arrived at work in the morning. And after a tough day of hard work, the ride home would help me erase everything, soothe my nerves, and put me in a great mood. How about that for taking the long way?

Understanding Speed Differential

If you can buy into the idea that it's not speed in and of itself that causes crashes, but the *difference* in speed that causes them, you understand a lot more than most people. In Chapter 12 we'll explore this area a little further, but for now, let's simplify and characterize this phenomenon with numbers. It will involve a little math and some minor leaps of faith, but in the end, the results will illuminate the relative risks involved with speed differential. Keep in mind that this is not meant to measure risk, only illustrate it.

Being too familiar with a route or a type of road can make you overconfident, lazy, or even apathetic toward surprises. That said, when you're at risk for another reason—poor traction, rush-hour traffic, poor visibility, mental or physical fatigue, or stress—your safest bet is probably to stick with the route you know best.

Deviant Speed*	Average Speed	Differential
90	30	27
90	45	18
60	20	18

*Deviant refers simply to the driver who's doing something different than everyone else.

The larger the speed difference between the fastest and the slowest driver on any given roadway, the larger the risk of a crash.

This can be used in other ways to measure relative risk. Where above I've alluded to you traveling at a certain speed above the speed limit, you can also use the same formula to estimate your risk based on someone else traveling a certain speed above or below the speed limit. The differential and the formula don't care who does what; they only look at the speeds and spit out an arbitrary calculation. Ask yourself, what's the biggest risk to you, the rider: 1.You traveling faster than (or the same speed as) the flow of traffic. 2. You traveling slower than the flow of traffic. 3. Someone else traveling faster than (or the same speed as) the flow of traffic. 4. Someone else traveling slower than the flow of traffic?

First, we'll assume two things:

1. The larger the speed difference between the fastest and the slowest driver on any given roadway, the larger the risk of a crash.

2. The higher the speed, the higher the rate of injury and death in the event of a crash.

Let's ignore most of the other variables for the time being, and give these assumptions some teeth so we can compare the risks.

Divide the higher speed by the lower speed: H/L. This will give you an idea of how much greater the higher speed is than the lower speed. Some arbitrary numbers:

30-mph zone: high 50 mph,
low 15 mph = 50/20 =
3.3 times greater
65-mph zone: high 80 mph,
low 40 mph = 80/40 =
2 times greater
15-mph zone: high 25 mph,
low 15 mph = 25/15 =
1.6 times greater
55-mph zone: high 55 mph,
low 55 mph = 55/55 =
1 (no factor)

Generally speaking, the closer the factor is to 1 (the smallest possible using this model), the less risk exists due to speed differential. Keep in mind this assumes everyone is more or less going the same direction and not pulling out into moving traffic from a standing start. Changing the lower speed to zero makes it kind of difficult to measure, so I've left it out—but keep in mind that someone turning from a stop in front of you is a bigger risk than someone traveling only 10 miles per hour slower than you!

Now we need to take into account the severity of the consequences of a crash as they're related to speed. For this, we'll assume that that injuries (and deaths) will be more severe (and more common) at 20 miles per hour than at 10 miles per hour, more severe at 40 miles per hour than at 30 miles per hour, a lot more at 50 miles per hour than at 20 miles per hour, more at 70 miles per hour than at 60 miles per hour, and a lot more at 70 miles per hour than at 30 miles per hour. Let's make this factor worth 10. Divide the speed at which the faster vehicle is traveling by 10, and then multiply that by the original factor of H/L. This gives you (H x H) / (L x 10). From the above examples:

50/15, 3.3 x 5 [50/10] =
Speed Differential 16.5
80/40, 2 x 8 [80/10] =
Speed Differential 16
25/15, 1.6 x 2.5 [25/10] =
Speed Differential 4
55/55, 1 x 5.5 [55/10] =
Speed Differential 5.5

Based on this model, measuring the difference in speed and the effects of speed on

Deviant Speed*	Average Speed**	Differential	Differential YOU	Differential
90	30	27	27	81
90	45	18	18	64
60	20	18	18	64
90	60	13.5	13.5	40.5
60	30	12	12	36
30	60	12	24	48
60	75	9.33	18.66	37.33
90	90	9	9	27
60	45	8	8	24
30	45	6.6	13.6	27.2
60	60	6	6	18
30	15	6	6	18
30	30	3	3	9

*Deviant refers simply to the driver who's doing something different than everyone else.
**Average simply refers to the flow of traffic.

*Assuming You+Fast=1, You+Slow=2, They+Fast=3, They+Slow=4

This isn't meant to be exhaustive or taken literally. It is interesting to note how relative speed, combined with absolute speed, combined with the fact (as is assumed throughout this book) that it's the other guy who's going to cause you the most trouble, can help you set your priorities.

injury severity and fatality, it appears that traveling 50 miles per hour in a 30-miles-per-hour zone has a pretty high risk level—16.5, more than four times the risk faced when traveling at 25 miles per hour in a 15-miles-per-hour zone. It also appears that going 80 in a 65 is only marginally more risky than going 50 in a 30. Additionally, going 55 in a 55 zone is only barely more risky than traveling 25 in a 15. Take a look at the relative risks associated with the speed differential equation.

All other things being equal, I'd guess that the other driver traveling slower than the rest of the traffic is the biggest risk—not necessarily that particular driver, but the others who will risk your life trying to get around them.

Your next biggest risk is the other driver who's traveling faster than the rest of the traffic. He or she is the one that's going to tailgate, weave, change lanes, drive on the shoulder, or generally try to force their way through the flow and force others to accommodate them. Here, your risks are

slightly less, but they now come from both the perpetrator and those trying to get out of their way.

Your third biggest risk is probably you traveling slower than the rest of the traffic. You're more difficult to see and more vulnerable, and people are less likely to give you the space you need when trying desperately to get around you to go on and wait at the next stoplight!

Of *these four*, probably the least risk lies in you traveling faster than the rest of the traffic, but remember that with increased speed comes increased risk, and possibly the ire of the local enforcers. You will also encounter additional risky situations as you progress through the other vehicles as well as new and interesting variations in driving ability and habit. You also introduce your own speed differential by riding faster than those around you. Ideally, your safest way to travel is at the same speed as the rest of the traffic, but this assumes that everyone else is traveling at the same speed. Since this is a factor beyond your control, you might consider traveling slightly faster than other traffic during high-risk times.

Rating the four possibilities of who's traveling faster or slower than the traffic is highly subjective and will differ greatly among motorcyclists, depending on their perception of the risks involved. You should decide for yourself which method is safest, but for kicks, how about we now assign each possibility a number to represent the least risk and most risk, say, 1 through 4, and multiply that by the speed differentials in the first table.

Before You Hit the Road
- Remember, speed changes everything.
- Take the road less traveled.
- Ride at, or slightly faster than, the speed of the rest of the traffic.

All other things being equal, I'd guess that the other driver traveling slower than the rest of the traffic is the biggest risk— not necessarily that particular driver, but the others who will risk your life trying to get around them.

GOOD TIMES, BAD TIMES

Are you a morning person or an evening person?

If you lived in Third Shift, New Jersey, would you be more cautious riding to work in the morning or riding home in the evening? If you lived in Strip Bar, Wisconsin, would you avoid riding at 1:00 in the morning? What about Factory, Illinois? What time of day is your favorite?

In every country, every province, every state, and every city, there are good times to travel and bad times. Put another way, there are high-risk times and *really* high-risk times. To know when most crashes happen and to hazard guesses as to *why* will put you at less risk. Are motorcyclists more likely than other drivers to crash, and if so, when are the most risky times?

Let's start with some inductive reasoning. What time of year would you guess that most crashes happen? I'd say winter, when roads are more often slippery and unmanageable. But what time of year would you guess that most motorcycle crashes happen? Now I'd say summer. Good weather equals more miles traveled equals more crashes.

In the United States, 4.9 million motorcycles represent 2.2 percent of all vehicles and 0.7 percent of all crashes.

So which day of the week would you guess that most crashes happen? I'd guess Monday, or maybe Friday. But which day would you guess most motorcycle crashes happen? Now I'm leaning toward Saturday, but Friday's still a good choice. Weekend, anyway. Now, factor in alcohol, and ask yourself which day of the week most alcohol-related crashes occur—now you're definitely thinking Saturday. Well, weekend, anyway. How about alcohol-related motorcycle crashes? Probably no different.

What about time of day? What time of day do you think most crashes occur? I'm guessing evening rush hour—say, 5 p.m. What about motorcycle crashes? I'm still thinking evening rush hour. What about alcohol-related motorcycle crashes? Now I'm thinking closing time.

These are all guesses purposefully based only on anecdote and prejudice. You may not agree with them based on your latitude, your perception of risk, or your personal experience. It doesn't matter. What does matter is that crashes are predictable to some degree. Every geographical area has its own trends and knowing them can help you avoid being, uh, trendy.

Statistics don't apply to anyone, but they do apply to everyone. Equally. If there are 1,000 crashes in your state every year, and 100,000 motorcycles, you have about a 1 in 100 chance of crashing

during any given year. So does everybody else. If half of all those crashes involve alcohol, and you don't drink, your odds just went up to 1 in 200. If half of all *those* crashes happened at night, and you never drink *or* ride in the dark, now your odds are up to 1 in 400. You see where I'm going with this.

What I'm saying is learn the stats. Know what the trends are in your state. They're probably pretty similar to statistics in other states, so the knowledge will help you in more locations than one. Included at the end of this chapter are instructions on obtaining this information for yourself.

Let's take a look at some national statistics and then a look at some local numbers, just to get a feel for it. We'll also make some leaps and draw some conclusions, just for fun.

Crashes

On the surface, it's easy to conclude that motorcyclists crash less but are more likely to be killed. Nationally, there are about 4.9 million registered motorcycles, accounting for 2.2 percent of all registered vehicles. (Most of the total of 220,480,600 registered vehicles are cars, light trucks, and large trucks.) But motorcycles account for 0.7 percent of the reported crashes, 5.6 percent of fatalities, 1.5 percent of injuries, and 0.2 percent of property damage crashes.

If you were to guess when most motorcycle crashes happen, what would your guess be? Which month do you think has the highest risk? What day of the week? What time of the day? Are most motorcycle crashes due to other drivers or the rider himself or herself? Do you avoid riding on certain days or during certain time periods?

Passenger cars and light trucks account for 94.9 percent of all reported crashes, with large trucks accounting for an additional 3.8 percent. This would imply that motorcycles are underrepresented in crash and injury statistics, but obviously overrepresented in fatalities.

Miles Traveled

Riders are definitely in the minority, and on first glance, based on their low rate of reported crashes, they appear to be better-than-average drivers. But the crash involvement when you look at miles traveled and crashes-per-registered-vehicle tells another story.

When you look at the number of miles traveled, motorcycles have a much higher involvement rate in fatal and injury crashes. This makes sense because across much of the country motorcycles disappear for months at a time. Motorcycling tends to taper off in the colder months. Motorcycles are also less often used for work and commuting, especially in northern climes.

Upon closer inspection, the differences are staggering. Motorcycles are 14 to 19 times more likely to be involved in a fatal crash and 4 to 13 times more likely to be involved in an injury crash. It is interesting to note that in crashes with only property damage, motorcycles show the least involvement of any vehicle. This is probably

Taking into account the lower number of miles motorcycles travel overall, it turns out riders are far more likely to be killed or injured out there—as much as 19 times more likely.

at least in part due to the vast number of motorcycle crashes that go unreported.

Registered Vehicles

In addition to looking at overall crashes and crashes in respect to miles traveled, we also need to understand how we compare to other vehicles. Looking at the actual number of vehicles on the road, motorcycles are overrepresented when it comes to numbers of crashes per mile traveled. Motorcycles are only slightly more likely than large trucks to be involved in a fatal crash, though they're two to three times more likely to be involved in a fatal crash than a passenger car or light truck. For injury crashes, motorcyclists have only slightly higher involvement than large trucks, but less than for passenger cars and light trucks. For property-damage crashes, motorcycles are beginning to approach their actual representation in the traffic mix and account for only about 2.6 percent of those crashes, but again, it is likely that a great number of these crashes go unreported.

When compared to all crashes and all registered vehicles, it's most realistic to gauge motorcycle safety by miles traveled. From that point of view, we see that not only are motorcycles more likely to be involved in a crash than other vehicles, but motorcyclists are definitely more prone to injury and death. Most motorcyclists

Crash Involvement per 100 Million Vehicle Miles Traveled

	Passenger Cars	Light Trucks	Large Trucks	Motorcycles
Fatal	1.73	2.13	2.31	34.1
Injury	144	125	43	594
Property Damage	278	275	161	152

Crash Involvement per 100,000 Registered Vehicles

	Passenger Cars	Light Trucks	Large Trucks	Motorcycles
Fatal	21.31	26.23	61	66.26
Injury	1770	1541	1143	1155
Property Damage	3418	3392	4261	295

Motorcycles only log 0.4 percent of all vehicle miles traveled. They have a much higher involvement rate in fatal and injury crashes.

This sign is posted on a nearly unavoidable road for those who have a cabin up north.

understand this at some level. They understand they're sacrificing the relative safety of a lawn chair or the steel cage of a four-wheeled vehicle for the freedom, fun, sunshine, fresh air, and challenge of riding a bike. Is there anything else we can learn from crash statistics?

Single or Multi-vehicle?

What's causing all these crashes? Nationally, about half of all motorcycle crashes involved another vehicle—54 percent in 2001. The other half involved only the motorcycle or the motorcycle and some other fixed or unfixed object. This is mostly unchanged from the time of the Hurt Study. However, I've found that in Minnesota, the rate of single-vehicle crashes to multivehicle crashes is closer to two to one. Unskilled riders, or riders who ride beyond their abilities, add a lot to those crash numbers. This tells me that in my own state, a rider who knows what he or she is doing, pays attention to training and skills and mindset, avoids drinking and riding, and takes steps to avoid things like sunburn and hypothermia has an above average chance of making it through a season unscathed. If I take the two-thirds of Minnesota riders involved in single vehicle crashes out of my own personal equation, my 33 percent chance of a multi-vehicle crash is far better than the national average of 50 percent. That's a significant risk reduction.

The When and the When

When are these crashes happening? For all vehicles—cars, trucks, motorcycles,

etc.—the month of September was the worst nationwide for *fatal* crashes, and the time period of July through December overall had the vast majority of fatalities.

High-speed summer driving, vacationing, and holidays could account for the high rate of summer deaths. Drivers relearning what cold weather and slippery roads are like at the onset of every winter could have something to do with the fall and winter deaths. Motorists in late fall have gone for several months without worrying about traction, and it takes time and a couple of sudden, scary practice slides to remember to slow down.

On the other hand, December accounted for the greatest number of *non-fatal* crashes, and the time period of October through March had the majority of non-fatal crashes. It's interesting to note the difference in the frequency of the type of crashes. The warmest months and the months of first snowfall give us most of the fatalities. The colder months and those with the most snowfall give us the most crashes overall. Could the changing of the seasons, fall for fatalities and spring for crashes, have anything to do with crash likelihood? On a primitive scale, the coming of winter means shorter days, preparation, hunkering down, and making sure everything's squared away for darker months. The coming of spring means going outside for pleasure again, longer days, and mating season. When the seasons are changing, where is human attention focused?

This is somewhat different from the specific monthly statistics in Minnesota, which showed that the month of August was the worst for fatalities, though the time period of July through December overall had the vast majority of fatalities. Think summer vacations, summer holidays, and lake homes. The month of February accounted for the greatest number of crashes, and the time period of October through March had the majority

Fatal crashes start to peak after 6 p.m. Injury crashes prevail from 9 p.m. to midnight, but the midnight to 3 a.m. shift is the prime time for deaths. This is no big surprise, as people are generally not sequestered at their jobs and are instead out having fun, out to dinner, taking in a happy hour, picking the kids up from the ice arena, or driving anxiously to home-improvement warehouses. Driving plays second fiddle to the destination, and this lack of attention combined with the end-of-day fatigue lends itself to an increase in crashes.

Bar closing time is simply a bad, bad time to be on the road, no matter what your skill level, state of mind, location, or choice of vehicle. Besides that, it's usually pitch black outside. Incidentally, no matter how much fun I'm having, when riding in Wisconsin on Sundays during football season, any driver wearing a green and yellow shirt or hat gets a wide berth from me. I take no chances with sports fans on game days.

of crashes. Think snow, the holiday season, the short days of winter, and the excitement of spring approaching.

Motorcycle crashes, however, concentrate more during the warm months of April through September. Crashes are rare or nonexistent in Minnesota and many other parts of the country from December through March. On the other hand, June, July, and August are the prime time for deaths and injuries. The unofficial start of the motorcycling season, Memorial Day, and the unofficial end, Labor Day, bookend the vast majority of motorcycle accidents. You can tell from the statistics when all the part-time, unaware, uninformed riders come out of the woodwork. There is also generally more traffic during these times, families vacationing, backyard barbecue parties, trips to the beach, you name it. The coincidence of more motorcycles on the road along with more road users creates an atmosphere ripe for more motorcycle crash incidents.

Does the time of day make a difference? Sure it does. Looking again at all vehicles across the country, crashes involving injuries vary little from hour to hour and fatal crashes begin to spike after 6 p.m. Injury crashes peak from 9 p.m. to midnight, but midnight to 3 a.m. is the prime time for fatalities. This is no big surprise, as people are generally not sequestered at their jobs and out having fun, taking the kids to soccer practice, or running to the home-improvement warehouses. Driving is secondary to the destination, and this lack of attention and also the end-of-day fatigue lends itself to an increase in crashes.

In Minnesota, however, crashes and fatalities peaked during the afternoon rush hours of 2 p.m. to 6 p.m., especially on Fridays and Mondays. This tells me that close to home, the chore of getting home from work is too much for the average driver, and their attention to detail and perception of risk are very poor. At these times, a driver's plans for the weekend,

memories of the previous weekend, or getting home in time to eat yummy frozen food in front of prime-time television, coupled with the distracting grind of work, play a large part in the increased incidences of traffic mishaps for property damage, injury, and death. This is an important point for the motorcycle commuter to remember, and I'll come back to it in a minute.

More motorcyclists are killed on the weekends, but more riders are injured on the weekdays. In 2001, weekdays accounted for about 48 percent of the fatalities and about 57 percent of the injuries. Weekends, by contrast, accounted for 52 percent of the fatalities and 43 percent of the injuries. The lion's share of motorcycle crashes happen between noon and 9 p.m., although for fatal crashes that time period extends to midnight. The overall 3 to 6 p.m. time period is the most hazardous for all injury crashes, although the 6 p.m. to 9 p.m. weekend period is the worst for fatal crashes. This isn't so hard to believe, as much of motorcycling is recreational in nature, and many, many riders use their bikes for fun in the evenings and on week-ends. And if you're going to die, it's likely that it will happen in the evening or at night.

In comparison, I found that an inordinate number of all motorcycle fatali-ties in Minnesota from 1998 to 2001 happened between 7:30 p.m. and 1:30 a.m., and the lion's share of the crashes happened between 2 p.m. and 6 p.m.; Friday, Saturday, and Sunday all have about

After a long day in the sun, on the lake, how focused on good observation, hazard detection, and safe driving are these people? Knowing where and why increased risk manifests itself is half the battle of safe motorcycling.

Drinking and driving (and riding) in the upper Midwest seems to be some sort of competitive sport, and after dark, after a long day of whatever, a motorcyclist's risks go way, way up.
Pat Hahn

1 1/2 times the number of crashes as a weekday. This is probably due to the recreational nature of motorcycling, especially in Minnesota, and the greater number of riders out there on the weekends. Drinking and driving (and riding) in the upper Midwest seems to be some sort of competitive sport, and after dark, after a long day of whatever, a motorcyclist's risks go way, way up.

Do you see a common thread among any elements here?

A friend of mine recently crashed his motorcycle in a low-drama single-vehicle event. Long story short: he's a skilled and conscientious sport-riding enthusiast. Last summer, he was carving corners with a friend over the border in the place we Minnesotans affectionately refer to as "Alphabetland," the county roads in Wisconsin marked with letters like O, Z, M, N, T, and D. The morning went fine, he felt good, in control; he was *on*. After lunch, they switched the lead and continued at the same pace. Shortly thereafter—very shortly, in fact—Mr. Gixxer had an unplanned get-off. Looking too long into his mirror for his comrade, a sharp corner snuck up and bit him. Hard.

Changing Gears

Think back to the Hurt Study. Remember that *50 percent of all motorcycle crashes happen within the first six minutes* of

riding. Why do you suppose that is? Why do you suppose such a large majority of crashes happen during rush hours? Aside from the obvious increased traffic volume, might there be another factor?

Let's approach this from a fresh angle. When you spend a long time inactive—being lazy, sitting down, studying, sleeping, whatever—and then decide to go walking or running or biking, how long does it take to get warmed up? When you start exercising, how many minutes does it take to get your heart pumping, to get your body burning fat? How long does it take to forget about what you *were* doing and focus on what you *are* doing? When you take a vacation, how many days does it take for you to forget about work and really start having fun? When you come back, how many days does it take to get back into the work groove? How about after a busy weekend of fun? How many hours or days does it take to get back down to business at work? After sleeping for eight hours, how long does it take you to wake up? I refer to this phenomenon as changing gears. It's the time of energy inefficiency between one mode of thought and action and another.

Example: you go on vacation. You get up early, you go to the airport, you fly to your

Riding in traffic has risks all its own. What do you suppose is the biggest risk on this road?

It's simply too great a mental task to go from one mode of thinking immediately to another. The last activity is difficult to let go, and the next one starts to intrude before you're ready. Driving home from work, people mull over the day's events while simultaneously thinking about what's going to be on the table for dinner. They think about the garage that needs to be cleaned and the cold beverage they're going to have while they're cleaning it. They think about getting to the auto parts store before it closes and helping their child on a project for the upcoming science fair. It all creeps in, takes away what little concentration that person might have had, and makes them a menace to themselves and everyone else on the road. It ain't pretty, but it's real.

In horror movies, zombies, moving in their slow and steady way, eventually ensnare all the living humans they can get their hands on. When sharing the road with zombies, understand that they will probably find a way to try to include you in their life.

It's not possible to avoid the process of changing gears. But it is within your control to shorten it or lessen its impact in an effort to put your mind where it needs to be—on the bike, on the road.

destination. You get to your new place, you check into your hotel or take a cab to your friend's house, and you sit down. So far it's all been a blur. You've been busy all day, and it's like a dream. You're a machine, going through the motions. You've accomplished a whole lot of nothing. You've put on miles and that's all. A whole day has passed, and you haven't felt it.

The next day, you get up and start having fun. But you're not *good* at it yet—you're still energy inefficient. The bed is unfamiliar, the sink, the stairs, breakfast. It's all fine, but you're still a little disoriented because it's so different. You feel like you should be at work, but you're not. (Part of you *is* at work.) You might even imagine what everyone else is doing—going to work, talking about you not being there, and so on. You might as well be there. You're still in work mode. But you're on vacation, you've already paid your money, so you push on.

You have your fun, whatever it might be—golf, beach, sightseeing, snorkeling—and you start to loosen up, imperceptibly. Your inputs for the last 24 hours have been entirely unrelated to work, and you begin to get into the groove. The next day you really tuck in and start having fun. You feel rested. You feel good-natured. You're on *vacation*. By day four, you're *down*. It's all good. You're finally where you wanted to be.

The problem is that it took *four* days. The transition alone cost you four vacation days. They weren't bad days, but because you were still in the work mode and weren't able to give them your full attention, you didn't get your full value for your dollar.

Everything's like that. Vacations. Mondays. Exercise. Sleep. When you change gears, when you switch from one mode to the other, you lose efficiency at both for a time. It's very difficult to concentrate on one when you're still in the cloud of the other.

So you lose efficiency and concentration changing gears. Big deal.

The reason it's important to the risk-averse motorcyclist is that if you're on the road changing gears, or if you're on the road while everyone else is changing gears, you're at a higher risk. This is probably why rush hour is so deadly. Not only are you and everyone else in a work-induced haze at 5 p.m. when the whistle blows because you're trying to switch from worker-bee gear to

dinner-TV gear, but you're also in the saddle or at the wheel. And what's worse, you have to switch gears *twice*, once from work to road and then again from road to home.

It's too much to ask a person to go from one thing to another. The last mode always lingers, and the next one starts to creep in. You start thinking about the leftover pizza that's in the fridge. The lawn that needs to be mowed. The cold beer you're going to have after you mow it. Throwing the football with your kid. Playing on the floor with your dog. It all creeps in, takes away the little concentration you do have, and makes you a menace to yourself and to everyone else on the road. It ain't pretty, but it's real.

The Solutions

How to solve the problem of changing gears? It's not easy. But like everything else, simply being aware of human weakness and being aware of the heightened risk is a good start. You might arbitrarily take fewer chances or drive slower or more defensively. You might force yourself to allow a greater margin of error. Knowing you're not at peak efficiency may also help you in your decision-making process.

David Hough, a very proficient motorcyclist, also suggests a solution: match your brain speed to the road speed. Just like matching your motorcycle's speed to the environment, make sure that your brain is able to deal with hazards at the rate at which they come. If they come too fast, you either have to speed up your brain (through focus and concentration on the task at hand) or slow down the rate at which the hazards approach (reducing your speed so your brain can keep up). This technique, used when changing gears, can save your biscuit.

Knowing that most everyone else is in the same boat is the second most critical point. I get annoyed at the bonehead maneuvers other drivers pull on my way to work, but then I think, "What do I expect?" I'm not totally on my game that early, either—and I'm one of the conscientious ones. For most people, driving doesn't even exist—the car is just the mode of transport that gets them all too soon to the place they'd rather not be anyway. Of course they're going to make dumb mistakes when they're tired. You need to be ready for people to be distracted, to make sudden unpredictable moves, to be somewhere else entirely. Just being aware of that lowers your risk.

Can we avoid changing gears? I doubt it. I don't think it's possible to eliminate the gear-changing period between modes. But you can shorten it or try to get most of it out of your system before you hit the road.

A leisurely period of walking to the bike, putting on your jacket and helmet, and taking slow, deep breaths all work to get your motorcycle juices flowing. What does a fighter do before going into the ring? Or a surgeon before heading off to the operating table? Maybe a prayer. Maybe a cigarette, or a glass of water. You need some kind of ritual to soak up some of the time you need to change gears and give your mind that extra time to adjust and focus. Let the bike warm up for a couple extra minutes. Give it a relaxed safety inspection. Focus on the task at hand. Maybe even sit on the bike without moving, visualizing the ride home—which way you're going to take, what you'll see, where the lights are, the trouble spots—and about what time you'll get home. Talk to yourself. Remind yourself that you're done working, you'll be home soon, but right now it's time to *ride the bike*. You can't avoid changing gears, but you can get good at it.

Do Your Own Research and See How Your State Compares

If you are interested in seeing the national traffic safety facts, reading up on motorcycle studies and reports, or pursuing the crash statistics in your own state to see how they compare with the rest of the country, several resources are available to you.

The National Highway Traffic Safety Association (www.nhtsa.gov) and the National Center for Statistics and Analysis have quite a bit of information available both on the national and state level.

The Governors Highway Safety Association (www.statehighwaysafety.org) is the states' voice on highway safety and is another good resource for traffic safety facts. Formerly the National Association of Governors' Highway Safety Representatives, *this* nonprofit association represents the highway safety programs of states and territories on the "human behavioral aspects" of highway safety. The GHSA web site has links to most states' transportation, motor vehicle, or safety agencies that report crash statistics.

Before You Hit the Road
- Know when and where crashes happen in your area.
- Know your mental and emotional limitations.
- Know the mental and emotional limitations of those around you.
- Force yourself to take the time you need to change gears.
- Self-assess: Learn to concentrate, no matter when or where or what.

"Hey old man, wanna race?" "Sure—how about to Denver?"

Does age play a part in risk? You bet it does. How invincible does a person feel at age 25? How invincible does the same person feel at 45? What is the level of shameless self-indulgence during a person's twenties as opposed to his or her thirties? Does being single or married, having kids or not, having good credit and a house and a job make a difference in rider behavior, or more specifically, a rider's likelihood to be involved in a crash? Insurance companies sure think so. Does aging's effect on vision, attention, coordination, reflexes, and confidence make a difference?

Recent studies show clearly that younger riders are still overrepresented and older riders are underrepresented in traffic fatalities. However, due to the changing demographics of the average motorcycle rider and the onset of increased baby-boomer free time, as well as the greater availability of safety training and alcohol awareness, younger riders are crashing less and older riders are crashing more. Younger riders are still more likely to crash than older riders, but the times are a-changing.

VISIBILITY

Maybe it's time to rethink this whole idea of "see and be seen."
Who's less likely to run into trouble, the rider who can see others well, or the rider who *others* can see well? Who's less likely to have a crash, the rider with superior visual skills or the rider who's highly conspicuous? Combining these into an effective visual arsenal is the best choice, but which would you choose if you had to choose between the two? Would you have a preference?

Let's look at it from the perspective of crash statistics. It's not unusual in any given year that half of the crashes are single-vehicle events. These single-vehicle crashes, i.e., those involving only the motorcycle, almost always draw their contributing factors from rider error. It's conceivable that another motorist could cause the crash without being involved in it. That happens all the time, to be sure. But even then, the rider still plays a major role in who's at fault. Since we've already established that every crash is the responsibility of the rider, it's only fitting to analyze a rider's self-control and skill at detecting risks—those posed by the rider, the environment, and other drivers. The role that vision—the motorcyclist's—

Can you see the rider in this picture? Shadows and reflections can tell you things that might not be obvious.

plays in whether a rider makes it home without having to use the old J.B. Weld or ending up in the bushes is most critical in reducing risk.

Among other things, such as poor skills when reacting to another motorist's gaffe or poor reactions to a surprise curve in the road, rider error can always be partially attributed to a poor understanding of the risks. While that seems to go without saying, it continues to beg the question of who, or what, is at fault. Take it further and see that a poor understanding of the risks can often be attributed to poor perception of the risks, which can in turn be attributed to poor observation of risks and hazards, which can stem from—yeah, you guessed it—poor vision or poor visual skills. Attitude can play a bigger part here, but this chapter is about visibility, so we'll leave that alone. So if half of the crashes can be partially attributed to poor vision or visual skills, rather than poor conspicuity, then the rider's ability to see is obviously the more important of the two.

But then again, single-vehicle crashes aren't a huge majority—and some years are not a majority at all. Generally, single-vehicle events comprise between 45 and 55 percent of all the crashes. That leaves 45 to 55 percent of the crashes being multiple-vehicle events, in which someone else shares the consequences with the rider. What causes a multivehicle crash? Not surprisingly, the rider and the driver share the blame. And yes, many times these types of crashes happen because the other driver just didn't see the rider. But are there instances in which the driver did see the rider and either didn't care or didn't care enough to react in time? Perhaps he or she saw the rider but was unable to judge the rider's distance or speed or guess exactly just why the bike's blinker was flashing.

So where does that leave us? If 50 percent of the crashes are single-vehicle and almost entirely our own fault, and we also share half the blame for multivehicle crashes, this means we're looking at being more or less directly responsible in 75 percent of all the

crashes. And of the remaining 25 percent, the crashes that you can directly attribute to the other drivers, how many of those involve a driver that absolutely didn't see the motorcycle? My guess is somewhere in the range of half of them, tops. Many poorly informed and poorly skilled riders think of other drivers as their worst enemy. It turns out that the "other guy" is not as big of a threat as they think. In Minnesota, for example, multivehicle crashes in which the other driver failed to yield right of way only account for about 18 percent of all motorcycle crashes.

Remember that risk factors need to accumulate to cause a crash. Riding with your eyes closed, your risks would pile up in a hurry, wouldn't they? Your best defense against any particular risk is to be aware of it and deal with it before it becomes a problem. Your vision is the first and most effective link between the risk and your awareness of it.

If you buy into the argument that good visual skills are the most critical of all the methods of taking in information as you ride, then this brings us to the conclusion that preserving and making good use of our own vision is 75 to 90 percent of the visibility battle. Or, put another way, our own ability to see is *three to nine times* as important as others' ability to see us.

Look at it this way, who's more likely to survive: a rider with 20/20 vision and excellent visual skills, riding around dressed in camouflage on an army-green Kawasaki KLR, or one with 20/200 vision who just broke one of the lenses in his or her prescription glasses, even though he or she is dressed like the Easter bunny in hot pink on a fluffy yellow chick motorcycle? All else being equal, my vote goes to Rambo. It's easy to see that the rider has the most need for good vision. Good visual acuity will help you avoid 75 to 90 percent of the visibility-related risk factors.

It also bears mention that a conspicuous rider will reduce his or her risks as well. Heck, 10 to 25 percent is still 10 to 25 percent.

The ability to see clearly and well makes the most critical difference to a

If you buy into the argument that good visual skills are the most critical of all the methods of taking in information as you ride, then a rider's ability to see is three to nine times as important as others' ability to see them. Do you spend three to nine times as much attention on your visual skills as you do on your visibility to others?

Do helmets limit peripheral vision? Sort of. Yes and no. Yes, they limit vision in the peripheral fields of eight to nine o'clock and three to four o'clock if you turn your eyes right or left without turning your head. The problem is, you couldn't see much that way anyway, even without the helmet. Try it: without turning your head, look carefully at what's at eight and four o'clock. See what I mean? And no, looking straight ahead, you can see just as much peripherally with a helmet on as without. To get a good look at peripheral fields, you need to turn your head.

Good vision is to motorcyclists as oxygen is to earthlings.

skilled rider's survival. The ability of others to see you clearly is exceptionally important too, but is secondary to your own vision. The vast majority of information that you and others take in is visual. Alone, your eyes tell you everything you need to know about the road and the surrounding environment in order to put that bike where it needs to be at any given time. In traffic, your eyes tell you all these same things, except now they're telling you these things and they're telling you about objects that are big, heavy, and in motion.

Look at It this Way

Good vision is to motorcyclists as oxygen is to earthlings. (Having superior riding strategy is like water, and being highly visible, like food.) There are about a million things that can affect your ability to see and others' ability to see you. Understanding that and taking steps to remove obstacles to good visibility is one of the smartest, easiest, and most effective ways to reduce your risk. Your primary goal is to put as few layers, real or otherwise, between your eyes and that which you're trying to see. Your secondary goal is to put yourself either actively or passively at the center of attention of the vehicles that can cause you the most trouble.

Making the most of your vision on a motorcycle is easy, and controlling the quality of 75 to 90 percent of the visibility you need means a lot of safety for a minimal amount of effort. The less between you and the hazards you're trying to see, the better. This means that your lenses and face shield are clean and scratch free. This means that you take care of your face shield; clean it at every stop with a soft sponge or cotton cloth, soap, and water; replace it when it needs it; and carry a spare just in case. Cleaning your visor with tree products such as paper towels or napkins works well at first, but leaves millions of tiny scratches that team up to make your visor looking like etched glass. If you ride with a tinted shield, you definitely need to carry a spare in case you get stuck out after dark.

A current and accurate prescription for your glasses, if you wear them, is imperative. Age plays a part, too. Understand that your eyes begin deteriorating the minute you leave the womb. Some people may never have a problem with this, but others will. Also, the benefits of sunglasses (prescription or otherwise) or a tinted face shield cannot be overstated. Why subject your eyes to more sunlight and glare than you need? A quality pair of shades or a dark shield can

Always having something on hand that cleans a filthy face shield without leaving scratches is the mark of an intelligent, risk-averse rider. Some riders have also been successful using Pledge (yes, furniture polish!) and a washrag for cleaning. These same riders, when asked if they ever get a waxy build up using this product, roll their eyes and claim sarcastically that when that happens, they will switch to Endust.

make a huge difference in the amount of eye strain and fatigue a rider has to deal with after a long, sunny day in the saddle. Also consider the benefits of colored glasses that enhance contrast, such as yellow or amber. Plus, they look really cool.

Poor sleep habits, long days in front of the computer, chlorine pools, and paint fumes can all have negative effects on your vision. Perhaps not much, but perhaps enough to warrant that you need to adjust your riding style, attention to detail, or space cushion when you're aware that your eyesight may be compromised. But what about prescription drugs? You know, the ones that seem innocuous but actually say on the bottle, "Do Not Operate Heavy Machinery." Is a motorcycle a heavy machine?

Showing Your True Colors

All this rider-see aside, it would be stupid to think you can't also make a difference by making yourself more conspicuous. Sure, it may be only 10 to 25 percent of the whole picture, but that's still a whole lot of risk that you can take steps to minimize.

Your first and most important consideration is to be brighter than your surroundings, both in color and hue. Vibrant colors like those used to show receptiveness for mating or display aggression in the animal kingdom draw a lot of attention. White and orange seem to work the best, but any bright color will do—red, blue, yellow, green—the more obnoxious, the better.

Using your high beam during the day can add to your conspicuity, but you still need to dim your headlight when approaching other traffic. An even better idea is the use of modulators on your headlight and taillight. While a headlight that's constantly on is good because it's bright, draws attention to itself, and few other vehicles have them on during the day, it's even better when it's a headlight doing something that you don't see every day—flashing.

Well, "pulsing" is the right word for it. The key to the legality of the headlight modulator is that it "pulses" rather than "flashes," flashing being reserved for subway trench-coat types and emergency vehicles. A headlight modulator is designed to work only in the daylight hours and gets its conspicuity by pulsing high beam-low beam-high beam-low beam at a certain rate. Basically, it's like

Vision Enhancers: clean scratch-free face shield, current prescription eyeglasses, high-quality sunglasses, and rest. Vision detractors: bugs, dirty water, old prescription lenses, cheap sunglasses, age, and alcohol. I'm not even going to begin to tell you about the effects of alcohol on vision. Only two little words are needed for that can o' worms: "beer goggles."

Headlight Modulators are Legal Equipment.

From the Federal Motor Vehicle Safety Standards (FMVSS) 571.108, S7.9.4 Motorcycle headlamp modulation system: A headlamp on a motorcycle may be wired to modulate either the upper beam or the lower beam from its maximum intensity to a lesser intensity, provided that:

A. The rate of modulation shall be 240 +/- 40 cycles per minute.

B. The headlamp shall be operated at maximum power for 50 to 70 percent of each cycle.

C. The lowest intensity at any test point shall be not less than 17 percent of the maximum intensity measured at the same point.

D. The modulator switch shall be wired in the power lead of the beam filament being modulated and not in the ground side of the circuit.

E. Means shall be provided so that both the lower beam and upper beam remain operable in the event of a modulator failure.

F. The system shall include a sensor mounted with the axis of its sensing element perpendicular to a horizontal plane. Headlamp modulation shall cease [at night or in low light levels].

Even at night there are ways to make yourself visible to those behind you.

having a device that works in place of your thumb (leaving your thumb to work the horn and your mind to ride the bike) flipping the high beam on and off constantly as you ride. But even though the legal rate at which the modulator pulses is determined by the federal Department of Transportation, and even though their motor vehicle code specifically includes headlight modulators as legal equipment, many otherwise well-meaning law enforcement officers do not know this, nor will they believe you when you tell them.

I'm telling you, it's true. You may be forced to fight it out in traffic court, but you have the federal motor vehicle code to back you up. To my knowledge, not one state in the United States specifically prohibits motorcycle headlight modulators. If an officer is truly concerned for public safety, a well-reasoned and polite explanation of the design, use, and benefits of your headlight modification should keep you out of hot water. Besides, they're not expensive, they're easy to install, and go a long way to improving your visibility to the hazards approaching from the Harry Hurt fields of 11 to 1.

The list goes on and on, but you get the idea.

But wait, it gets better. You can also hook up one of these little beauties to your taillight. A simple device the size of a matchbox wired into your rear lens flashes the stop lamp every time you use the brakes. You squeeze, the light goes flash, flash, flash, or some combination of long and slow flashes designed to get attention. I don't know any conscientious riders who don't flash their brake light when coming to a stop in traffic. Why do they do that? Risk aversion. While rear-end crashes for motorcycles are very rare, they're not uncommon at stop signs and stop lights in urban areas. They're also not uncommon on two laners without turn lanes and on freeways when traffic stops suddenly.

Yellow-Light Management

Lightly dragging your brakes when approaching busy intersections on a yellow light—especially if you own a taillight modulator—puts you at a relative advantage and can greatly decrease your risk. For one thing, you flashily alert the vehicle behind you that you intend to stop and therefore they should too. Without any extra effort on your part, your rear lens lights up repeatedly as if you're speaking directly to that person, "Stopping! Stopping! Don't hurt me! Yellow light! Yellow light!"

It doesn't matter whether you intend to stop or not. You're keeping your options open. I'll tell you why.

By lightly fanning the brake, you're not only sending a strong signal to the driver behind you, but by braking only imperceptibly, you're also sending a message to the oncoming cars. "Coming through! Rider trying to clear the intersection! Please wait your turn! Right of way!" You're giving those ahead of you a reason to stop, at the same time you're giving the vehicle behind you a reason to stop. This leaves you the most possible options when deciding whether to stop for, or run, a yellow. You now have the option: You can stop or you can go. Note: Braking and dipping your headlight in heavy traffic is just *begging* for the Other Guy to make his or her move. Be careful about being too enthusiastic when covering your brakes.

But here's the rub: lightly using the

brakes to alert the driver behind you has more than one benefit. By dragging the brakes, you've already begun the process of stopping the bike. Part of the transition from moving forward to being stopped has been accomplished. The oncoming vehicle is your bigger risk factor, but in dragging the brakes you've also eliminated the half-second reaction time of getting your fingers to the lever, *and* you've begun to compress the forks and build traction on the front tire. Your bike is just *aching* for a quick stop, and you're ready for either stop or go. Your options are open. If one of the vehicles makes a bad move, *you* get to make the choice rather than being forced into one.

Being Invisible

I guess we can't have a discussion about being seen without giving a nod to "not being seen." It's okay to be invisible, as long as you're aware of the fact.

One of the primary tenets of visibility in the three degrees of separation is proper positioning in traffic. Savvy riders use the whole lane and the whole road to see others and to make themselves obvious. When you're in a situation where you suspect others can overlook you, take steps to change the situation by moving, slowing, speeding up, or getting out entirely by turning or exiting. Pay attention to the nagging voice that reminds you that someone probably can't see you.

It's your job to determine who these people are who don't see you. You can then either take steps to give them as much personal space as a rattlesnake at a bulbous ankle convention or make an effort to enter their field of consciousness through movement, positioning, or otherwise drawing attention to yourself. Honking your horn is one method of getting attention, a method that satisfies the New York taxi driver in all of us.

Fortunately, picking out the people who don't see you isn't too difficult. You see them merge with traffic without turning their heads, glancing furtively into their side-view mirror instead. You see them reading something really important or finding just the right mood music for the ride while their car is in motion. You can see the sun shining in their eyes. You can

see their passengers talking animatedly in the back seat, perhaps even movin' and groovin' or wrestling. You can see their out-of-state license plate and the gigantic eyesore of a tourist attraction looming somewhere on the horizon. You can see the happy summer driver with a drippy ice cream cone, or, believe it or not, you can see the circus sideshow lady steering with her *elbows* while eating, of all things, corn on the cob. I've honestly seen that.

Know Your Blind Spots

Sure, everybody knows that there's a place over either shoulder that you can't see. These places are extremely important when you're driving a car. But can the problem be solved with mirrors and head checks? Not always. We know not to ride in another vehicle's blind spot, but is there more we should know?

Take a look at the orientation of the mirrors on a car or truck. The rearview mirrors, typically high up and centered on the windshield, are usually pointed in the correct direction and give a broad view of the area behind the car in the range of about five to seven o'clock. In occasional instances, the four-wheeler in question is being driven by a makeup artist or someone obsessed with his or her face, but for the most part, most rearview mirrors are serving their intended purpose out there.

But what about the sideview mirrors? How often do they serve their purpose? In my experience, they are very seldom used correctly. Sideview mirrors are placed by the manufacturer to give the driver visual access to important areas that the rearview mirror can't show—the sides of the vehicle behind the doors but in front of the area shown in the rearview mirror at about the four and eight o'clock range. That's an important place to have access to, because humans cannot see those areas while facing forward. But where do half of America's road users aim their sideviews? Right back into the same zone as the rear view—sacrificing any advantage they could gain by using three different mirrors in which to see the exact same things.

Very few people use sideview mirrors to see the blind spots. I'd guess the number to be than 5 in 10 or fewer.

Braking and dipping your headlight in a busy intersection is an invitation for another driver to make his or her move. Be careful about being too enthusiastic when covering your brakes.

One of the pure rules of visibility in the three degrees of separation is proper positioning in traffic. Smart riders use the whole lane and the whole road to see and be seen. When you're in a situation in which you suspect others have overlooked you, immediately adjust your role in the situation by moving, slowing, speeding up, or getting out of the situation entirely by turning or exiting.
Pay attention to the little voice in your head that says, "You've been in one place too long, and you're invisible again. Time for a change."

79

The driver in this truck cannot see the motorcyclist, even with a proper head check.

View from the driver's seat.

Watch out for gray spots: heavily tinted windows that mute sunlight and reduce contrast, thereby creating an artificial blind spot.

Instead of only choosing your position based on the existing hazards, choose it based on imagined hazards as well. If the shoulder has a gravel surface and is not paved, you may want to adjust your line. If you have only one other lane to work with and no shoulders at all, take note of that fact. If it's all woods and dead deer, or hills blocking your view of oncoming, double-yellow-straddling tankers, keep track of all those things, and choose your lines accordingly.

Vanishing Act

Question: When is a blind spot not a blind spot? When an object in it is completely invisible.

There are some vehicles with blind spots that neither the mirrors (unless properly adjusted as above) nor an over-the-shoulder head check can help. There are easy ones to spot, such as vans without side windows, service trucks, moving vans, etc., but are there others?

Absolutely. The worst I've seen is the left-side B-pillar blind spot on late-model Ford Ranger extended cabs, the kind on which the rear half-doors open like the old suicide doors. The smallish size of the rear window and the width of the door frames block out areas large enough to fit a small car! Even with turning your head around to view the area squarely with both eyes, a motorcycle could easily fit in the blind spot. A person practically needs to stick their head out the window to see it. Of course, properly adjusted sideview mirrors can help solve this.

Convertibles with their tops up have incredibly large blind spots. So do the last generation of Ford Broncos—remember them, with the removable top? How about large, late-model sport utility vehicles with dark tinted windows? The shaded windows mute the bright, reflective surfaces of outside objects and can create gray spots. And the low seating position and sporty fastback styling of two-door cars like the Grand Am, Probe, RX-7, Prelude, and 300Z have large blind areas, too.

Another unexpected blind spot comes from the rearview mirror itself. In vehicles like sport utility vehicles and trucks, the driver sits up so high and the windshield is so small that the rearview mirror can block the driver's long-range view in the direction of about 1:30. This isn't such a big deal in close traffic, because the driver can still see clearly the vehicles close by. But wait until he or she comes to a cloverleaf. The mirror effectively blocks vehicles merging from the right. While actually on a right-turning on ramp or off ramp, the mirror also effectively blocks vehicles that the driver is about to merge with. While this mirror doesn't block out every merging vehicle all the time, it can easily block one motorcycle moving at a certain relative speed for the entire merging maneuver.

The Right Place at the Right Time

When choosing a lane or positioning your bike within your lane for maximum

Here we see the view through the windshield of a very common sport utility vehicle. There's nothing there, right? Au contraire—there is a motorcyclist about to assume her right of way while completely out of sight of the SUV driver. This rearview mirror design flaw is common and poses a huge threat to motorcyclists on cloverleaf ramps and in the hands of semaphore ignorers.

When riding in low, bright sunlight, choose a route that puts others at the disadvantage, rather than yourself, if you can. The only person truly concerned for your safety out there is you, and you will have more control over your surroundings by not riding directly into the sun. Take care, though, and keep in mind that this is only a small advantage. Riding during times like this is a huge compromise. You need to be supervigilant and remember that everyone else, for all practical purposes, is driving with their eyes closed.

visibility, consider too the escape route options your positioning leaves you in an emergency. Riding in the center lane of a three-lane highway offers you the most runout to either side—your own lane left and right, the lanes next to you left and right, and the left and right shoulders. (Of course, riding in the center lane also means that hazards can approach you from both directions, as well.) By riding in the center, you equalize the distance between you and each of these alternate paths, maximizing your options. Traveling in the left lane reduces your road space to the left, while traveling in the right lane reduces your road space to the right. Of course, this generally removes one direction from which a hazard could approach, too. It's a tradeoff, depending on where you feel more comfortable riding. If only one side of the road has a useable shoulder, take that into account. If the highway isn't divided, take that into account as well—traffic allowing, you have the opposite side of the road to work with if you need it.

Also think about how your position within your own lane affects your escape routes. Riding in the center oil stripe is generally a no-no, but be aware of how many escape routes you have to either side when you choose your lane position. If you have a shoulder to work with, note that. If the shoulder has a gravel surface and is not paved, note that. If you have only one other lane to work with and no shoulder, note that. If it's all woods and dead deer to one side, or if the hills block your view of oncoming, double-yellow-straddling tankers, note all those things, and choose your line accordingly. Instead of only choosing your position based on the existing hazards, choose it based on imagined hazards as well.

Troubling Times

Sunrise and sunset put about 25 percent of road users at a distinct disadvantage. If you happen to be on a road oriented directly toward the sun, make that about 50 percent. Fortunately in that case, you know who else is being blinded—either you and everyone else on your side of the road, or everyone on the other side.

During early morning or late evening hours, the quality and clarity of your eye

You can take steps to improve your own visual ability, but what steps can you take to improve others' visual ability? None? How about washing their windshields for them? Motorcycle riders in Minnesota and Illinois get together once a year at rest areas and gas stations and give free windshield washes to motorists. In addition to giving away safety information and putting a friendly face on motorcycling, they are also literally and figuratively helping people see motorcyclists better. See also Chapter 9. Courtesy Minnesota Department of Public Safety

If your vision is ever severely compromised– blocked by large-vehicle traffic, rendered useless by the sun, impaired by weather, whatever– remember who has had more than just "sign here, please" driver training. Paying attention to the actions of professional drivers–truck drivers, especially–might give you an extra edge and help you go with the flow.

protection—face shield, goggles, glasses— make a huge difference in your ability to detect hazards. If good vision is ever temporarily lost—blocked by traffic, glare from the sun, wrecked by weather— remember who else out there has been trained to drive safely. Paying attention to the actions of professional drivers—truck drivers, especially—might give you an extra edge and help you go with the flow when your abilities are compromised.

When you can, it's wise to choose a route that puts others at the disadvantage rather than yourself. You will have more control over your surroundings if you're not the one blinded and riding directly into the sun. Remember though, that this is only a small advantage, and riding during times like these is a huge compromise. Traveling in low-angle bright light, you must be supervigilant and remember that everyone else, for all practical purposes, is driving wearing blindfolds. Your positioning and preparation for intersections and other breaks in the flow of traffic need to be paranoid to say the least. Shadowing other vehicles through intersections is

highly advisable (see Chapter 10). Using your high beam or a headlight modulator is also a good way to help others notice you. And definitely don't expect anyone to take notice of what your brake light is doing, whether you're facing into the sun or not. Whether you're looking into the sun or having it stare at you through your mirrors, a brake light is a weak competitor for a million-degree flaming ball of hydrogen and helium. Be ready to jump forward at stop signs and stop lights, and do your best to make no sudden braking maneuvers.

Riding into the sun is generally a matter of choice—if you have no where to be at any particular time, you can always choose a different route. But what about commuting? You still have a choice to some degree, but it's generally limited. The best choice is to adjust your work schedule to travel earlier or later during the day. As the earth moves through its orbit and the angle of the sun changes through the seasons, you will generally only have to adjust your schedule for a couple weeks in the spring and a couple in the fall.

This is only amusing if you don't think about it too hard.

Crash-Causing Creatures

Overall driving activity in the late-evening, low-light, blinding-sun hours is different, too. During the work week, you're generally dealing with people who are done for the day and are either making their way home, running distracting errands like grocery shopping or carting around soccer players, or those who have stopped off for happy hour and are now more concerned with getting to the nearest bathroom than they are with actually driving the car.

Deer and other prey animals tend to move quite a bit during low-light times, especially during spring green up and the fall mating season. In heavily forested areas or along bodies of water, expect more large fuzzy creatures to be making their way across your path, searching for food or water or some companionship. When you see a sign indicating a deer crossing (How do they know to cross there?), understand that lots of deer crashes have happened in that area, and choose a different route or reduce your speed to accommodate more surprises.

The worst animal to come out at night is *homo sapiens cocktailus*. While the happy-hour crowd is high risk, the mixed-drinks-for-dinner-instead-of-food crowd is outright lethal. Just when vision is severely compromised by the onset of night, these ignorant fools have gone and compromised theirs even further by dumping a bunch of alcohol into their system. Expect their attention, perception, predictability, and decision making to be in the toilet along with their night vision. Extra attention at stoplights, stop signs, T-intersections, on the freeway, or anywhere else a drunk may have to pass through is an absolute requirement. In fact, just stay off the road altogether from about 9 p.m. until 5 a.m.

Before You Hit the Road:

- Your vision is more important than anything or anyone.
- Dress loudly.
- You're invisible.

The worst animal to come out at night is the drunk driver. Just when vision is severely compromised by the onset of night, these complete idiots have gone and compromised theirs even further by sucking down a bunch of cocktails. Expect their attention, perception, predictability, and decision making to be in the toilet along with their money, breath, and conversation skills.

chapter 7

RIDING AT NIGHT

DON'T RIDE AT NIGHT.

When in doubt, reread Chapters 5 and 6.

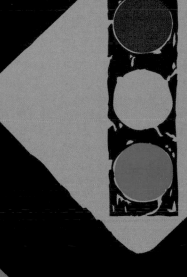

What's wrong with this picture? Too much is wrong with this picture. If you want to lower your risk, avoiding night riding is a close second to separating drinking and driving. When in doubt, reread chapters 5, and 6.

chapter 8

MAKE IT FAMILIAR

When faced with a bad situation, would you rather face it for the first time, or would you rather have faced it before? Which way affords you a greater margin of safety, the devil you know or the devil you don't?

If you're like me, you spend a great deal of your waking moments and almost all your working moments thinking about motorcycling. While you should be paying attention to your work, you're thinking ahead to hopping on the bike and taking the long way home. Instead of paying the bills, you're wondering what the consequences would be of putting them off for another day and taking advantage of the great cloudless motorcycle weather outside. Instead of listening to your better half or your mother tell you about her day, you're instead daydreaming of a blast through the countryside on your favorite machine. At any rate, you're not thinking about what's in front of you; you're thinking about motorcycling.

Maybe it's time to put that obsession to work for you.

Athletes understand the value of visualization and can use it to enhance their performance. Strong visualization practice and purposeful mental concentration can help them get closer to (impossible) perfection in their skills, moves, and reactions. Playing an active role n their imaginations, seeking out hypothetical situations, and mentally going through the response motions helps prepare them for the time when they may need to make those moves.

Visualization, a technique very useful in the game of golf, is also useful to a rider looking to save his or her skin.

Since When Does Golf Have Anything to Do with Motorcycling?

Take, for example, a professional golfer. Yes, believe it or not, they're athletes too. It's a lucky thing that riding a motorcycle skillfully isn't half as hard as putting a golf ball exactly where you want it. A professional golfer generally plays it safe by keeping some strength and strategy in reserve. They try to stick to the obvious path of travel and leave the fancy stuff for when they really need it. A skillful motorcyclist does the same, keeping some available space, traction, and attention in reserve for when it becomes invaluable. A professional golfer has some tricks that most motorcyclists don't have. But if a motorcyclist puts forth some effort, he or she can develop some professional-grade tricks that could very well save his or her life.

Know why golf is so boring on TV? Everything looks the same. The grass, the greens, the clothes, even the way the golfers hit the ball is the same. But beneath these observations lies another, more subtle, fact. Each golfer is swinging very, very differently from the others. Each player has his or her own strengths, weaknesses, dexterity, body type, energy level, concentration level, clubs, balls, you name it. Their individual ability to control the ball's distance and placement depends upon their exact perception, precise interpretation, and exact judgment. They must evaluate things like distance, wind, elevation, and surface conditions. They must use deliberate orientation, unerring posture, and follow an exact sequence of muscle memorization from setting up for the swing all the way through the ball and the follow-through.

Great golfers are able to swing a club naturally, but what makes them truly great is using their mind to hone their skills to a professional level. They work really hard when not competing to prepare their minds and practice overcoming every conceivable obstacle—before they have to do it to make the cut. They visualize not only the layout, conditions, and hazards, but also their actions within that environment. When the time comes to show their stuff, they're ready for that particular situation. They condition their mind and body to deal with whatever may come their way by making it familiar. And when they're out on the links and they're faced with a difficult shot, their mind has already seen it, already developed a solution to the problem, and they've practiced it until their body is conditioned to behave in the way they tell it to behave.

The technique of visualization can also work for motorcyclists. I'm not talking about the "What if?" game that we play to identify hazards in the riding environment. That's a fundamental part of the first degree of separation. In theory we've internalized that now and do it instinctively. I'm talking about dreaming up hazards and the environments in which they might happen, examining your options, and then visualizing yourself executing your decisions and your reaction to the situation.

Get the whole picture: See yourself in the cockpit of your bike. Your gloves, your jacket, your gas tank are all familiar sights. See yourself approach a situation, imagine all the possible outcomes, but then focus on one outcome and deal with it. See your hands and feet move in response, see your bike change position, speed, or direction to correct the situation, and see the hazard disappear in your rearview mirror. You can do this all from the comfort of your office, the passenger seat of a car, or your favorite ruminating chair. It's especially rewarding to do it when other people think you're listening to them.

By seeing these things before they happen, you break through the first mental barrier to perfect performance and road management. By practicing them from the safety of your imagination, you begin to develop conditioned responses to hazards that may or may not ever come your way. Being ready and familiar with even the most unusual situation gives you an edge when it comes to dealing with surprises. Being mentally well-practiced

When I discuss visualization, I'm not talking about the "What if?" game. I'm talking about thinking up bad situations and the worst environments in which they might happen and visualizing yourself using all the skills in your arsenal to save your bacon.

By seeing these things before they happen, you break through the first mental barrier to perfect performance and road management. By visualizing them from the safety of your imagination, you begin to develop conditioned responses to hazards that may or may not ever come your way.

You've just started downhill, bouncing at 35 miles per hour straight toward the next wash, when a deer pops out of the woodwork and stops—right in front of you.

conditions your body to react more in the way you want it to rather than in the way your instinct tells it to. Instinctive reaction can be a good thing, and it can also be a bad thing, especially on a motorcycle. Visualization practice can train your instincts to work for you and not against you. Just imagine the natural reaction of a newer rider who enters a corner too hot and decides to fixate on the guardrail. Bad instinct! Bad!

Finding Your Happy Place

So how does this visualization process work? Let me get you started. You're riding along a very familiar gravel road that is straight as an arrow but very hilly. Up, down, up, down.

The road is familiar to you, you are not uncomfortable with the surface (it was recently graded), and you regularly take it above the posted limit because there's never any traffic. You've just crested a hill, swooping down toward the next gully, leaving a terrific cloud of brownish red dust in your wake, when a deer jumps from the bushes on the left side and into the road.

From the comfort of your favorite hammock and fluffy pillows, imagine the worst, put yourself in the midst of it, and visualize getting it right and saving your banana. Use your imagination to train your instinct, condition your body, and prepare your mind with full knowledge that the right maneuvers will move you out of harm's way. Confidence and experience, even if they're artificial, will take you places you've never imagined.

Visualize yourself out of *this* one. Look at yourself as if you were watching from the passenger seat in this situation. There you are, with your helmet, your jacket, your gloves, the windscreen in front of you, the mirrors showing nothing but dust. See yourself using the front brake gingerly while aggressively digging the rear tire into the gravel in a controlled skid. Rumor has it that animals are scared of noises. If you were a deer, what would the sound of a skidding tire on gravel do to your desire to stand on the road?

Watch yourself as you scrub off speed and play your next move. Eyeing the deer carefully, both eyes focused on the animal, you wait for it to either jump again, stop, or turn. Now imagine that with its second leap the deer leaps directly into your former path, which you already adjusted after releasing the brakes, choosing instead to aim for the area of road just to the left of the deer's fluffy white tail. Now watch the deer bound into the bushes on the other side, and now see yourself gently steer the motorcycle back toward your previous path of travel, drifting a little bit to the left with both wheels as you use 100 percent of your traction to guide the bike away from the ditch. It makes me pucker up just thinking about it, but it worked. Know why? Because I *said* it did. If you see it work one time, no matter if you dreamed the whole thing or not, it's more likely that it will work for you when you need it.

How about another one? Now try it on a rainy city street at night. You can't see much, the droplets on your visor magnify the streetlights, the sound of the wet pavement hisses in your ears. You are very aware of the slippery pavement beneath you as you move along slowly through the wet night.

If you're someone who refuses to ride in the rain, you should get out there in the wet stuff some day to show your subconscious that it can be done. Putting on rain gear isn't always easy and takes a little practice. Understanding how your

If you're one of those wusscakes who refuses to ride in the rain, get out there during a soft summer rain some day to show your subconscious that it can be done. Rain gear isn't always user friendly, and it takes a little while to get used to it. Having your arm and leg movements restricted by rain gear may come as a bit of a surprise—be surprised when you want to, not when you have to. Learning to trust your tires on a wet surface is important for the time when you find yourself looking into the gaping maw of an unavoidable storm. Learn at your own pace; go out and do it on your own terms.

Your goal is to build up your immunity to "lane-o-phobia." It's easy to forget while we're trying to be good little bikers and assimilate into modern society that the roads we pay for are a lot wider than the lane within which we normally confine ourselves. There's a good deal of potential surface there for the taking. The roads are designed for it, and sometimes you have to know when to break the rules.

movements may be restricted by rain gear may come as a bit of a surprise. Learning that you actually have a good deal of traction and control, even on a wet surface, is important for the time when you find yourself looking into the gaping maw of an impending summer rain shower. Having to learn when you're least prepared to learn is risky and, frankly, not a lot of fun. Go out and do it on your own terms.

There's a cab riding along next to you. You notice it with wonder as it suddenly speeds up and then steadies in the other lane about two seconds in front of you. Suddenly, the driver decides to swerve into your lane, brake hard, and initiate a turn into a hotel drop-off. Take yourself through the steps of your reaction. Tell your hands what to do, tell your feet what to do, tell your bike what to do. Watch yourself from behind as you successfully avoid this hazard with room to spare, defying all odds. Get used to the idea that it can be done, memorize how you imagined doing it, and put it in your mental arsenal of "things to do on a rainy night in the city if I need to."

Visualize riding on a windy urban freeway in heavy traffic when a three-foot hunk of plywood or Masonite or dry wall or something flips up out of the bed of a truck and floats, not toward you, but toward the car immediately to your right. Visualize every detail, use your skills to dodge the bullet in your mind, and then memorize your reactions.

You see where I'm going with this? Imagine the worst, imagine every detail, put yourself in the saddle, and visualize successfully avoiding it. You're trying to train your instinct to react in the way that makes the most sense for the conditions. You're trying to condition your body and your mind to respond instantly and with full knowledge that the right maneuvers, practiced already in the easy chair, will place you out of harm's way. Confidence and experience, even if it's artificial, can take you places you've never imagined.

Athletes also understand the value of physical practice. This kind of practice builds muscle and endurance and helps your body develop the memory of the motions. Physical practice helps the motion become unconscious, instinctive, instantaneous. It helps you achieve a good

condition in which to participate in your sport of choice. Practice will never make perfect, but practice will usually make progress. Understand that visualization alone will not help you as much as visualization *plus* dedicated practice to the skills you need to perform critical maneuvers. So there you are. Practice your braking. Practice your swerving. Practice separating them. And practice your "What if?" game. These efforts refine and hone your first and second degrees of separation.

Technique Tip:
Ignore the Lines

Psychologically, you can increase your defensive arsenal too. Try this to begin with: When traffic and weather conditions allow it, make a deliberate, controlled slow-speed swerve across the white dashed line, and then back again to your position. Try this a few times, getting the feel for crossing the line. Then try it across a yellow dashed line. Get used to the idea of using the oncoming lane for practice. Then try it across a solid yellow centerline, and then across the solid white fog line and then onto the shoulder. At very low speeds, find a place with good footing and simulate swerving across a whole lane of traffic, braking hard in a straight line, and then gently driving off the road, over the shoulder, and into the grass where you're safely out of reach of the private aircraft making an emergency landing behind you. From a standing start, point your bars at the curb and quickly, carefully, slowly, surmount the curb and pull into someone's (probably should be your own) front yard.

The idea here is to build your emotional and psychological resistance to the fear of crossing the lines. Using public roads and remaining a fine, upstanding citizen has us confined at all times to our lane of traffic. (Well, except in Chicago.) To get over it you need to practice this stuff—a lot. Your goal is to build up your immunity to "lane-o-phobia." It's easy to forget while we're trying to be good little bikers and assimilate into modern society that the roads we pay for are a lot wider than the lane within which we normally confine ourselves. There's a good deal of potential surface there for the taking. The roads are designed for it, and sometimes you have to know when to break the rules. You've got an oncoming lane, adjacent lanes going your direction, shoulders paved or not at the sides, and grassy embankments that can support a moving motorcycle. In an emergency, you're not limited to just your one chosen lane. There is a whole great big slab of roadway for you to use. Imagine using it. Use it. Get used to using it all. Make it familiar. Visualize riding directly into oncoming traffic, riding on the shoulder, pointing your bike at a ditch, so if the time ever comes when you must make a choice between breaking the rules or facing certain death, it won't be the first time you've deliberately aimed a bike at a barbed-wire fence. You never know when that will become the day's preferred alternative.

Before You Hit the Road:
• Dream up impossible situations.
• Visualize them intensively.
• Practice them until they're familiar.
• Break the rules when you have to.|

If the time ever comes when you must make a choice between breaking the rules or facing certain death, it won't be the first time you've deliberately aimed a bike at a barbed-wire fence.

chapter 9

MAKING FRIENDS

Who poses more risk, the motorist who knows motorcyclists or the one who doesn't? Who poses more risk, the motorist who knows and likes motorcyclists, or the one who knows and dislikes motorcyclists?

Who is more likely to cause you trouble, a motorist who doesn't know a Hog from a Hayabusa or a motorist who does? Which would probably pose more risk to you, the person who has never, ever even met a motorcycle rider or the person who has?

This could go either way. Someone who neither knows nor cares about motorcyclists can be exactly what you want . . . or exactly what you don't want. It depends on the person. It depends on the situation. Chances are, though, that if they're exactly what you don't want, they're probably also what everybody else doesn't want, too. They're people who could care less about you and care less about driving. So they're probably bad news. But really, which is better, the devil who knows you or the devil who doesn't? This is a toss-up and depends almost entirely on the person who either knows or doesn't know about motorcyclists. It's hard to predict much more than that.

Start them young.
Pat Hahn

Ignition Motorsports' romantic battle cry may not work every time, but it never hurts to try.

But now ask yourself this: Of all the people who do know about motorcyclists, including maybe people who even know a motorcyclist personally, which ones are likely to cause you the most trouble, the ones who know and *like* motorcyclists or the ones who know and *dislike* motorcyclists? Now maybe it's a little clearer, a little more predictable.

Four Types of Other Guys

There are four types of road users out there we have to deal with:
- The ones who don't know much about motorcyclists and don't like them either.
- The ones who don't know much about motorcyclists but do like them.
- The ones who know about motorcyclists but don't like them.
- The ones who know about motorcyclists and do like them.

There will be varying degrees of knowledge and affinity, but every road user can be grouped into one of these categories.

Of the four choices, not knowing-not liking, not knowing-liking, knowing-not liking, and knowing-liking, it's best that other drivers both know about and like motorcyclists or at least know about and like a motorcyclist *somewhere*.

Think about it. Imagine you had the magical ability to transform nonriders' attitudes any way you wanted, and those were your choices, which would you choose for your own safety? Which attitude overall would mean the least amount of risk for riders? You would ensure that every other driver knows at least one motorcyclist personally and that he or she likes them. You would strive for a driving society that both knows and likes motorcyclists. True, the argument that a society that doesn't know and doesn't care might be preferable sometimes, but ultimately you are better off when your presence is prominent and positive.

So how can you help create a situation in which people know and like motorcyclists? What can you do to push the attitude toward that of less risk to riders?

Imagine that there are degrees to the amount of risk you face based on how someone feels about motorcyclists. The original four choices—know-like, not know-like, know-dislike, and not know-dislike—respectively represent increased

Which is better, the devil who knows you or the devil who doesn't? This depends on the person who either knows or doesn't know about motorcyclists. Which is better, a road user who knows about motorcyclists or one who doesn't?

When mounting your driveway or performing any low-speed maneuver with an audience nearby, make a real show out of slowing carefully, approaching at a right angle, pointing the bike up toward the garage, then gently easing the tires, first front, then back, over the curb. Not only can a show like this prove how careful you are, but it could also hint to someone that maybe motorcycles need a little extra attention when it comes to bumps in the road.

When a kid throws a snowball at your car it is your patriotic duty as an adult to slam on the brakes, whip the car onto the shoulder or into a driveway, get out, roar like an angry lion, and chase them. What fun is it for them if you just keep on driving? The thrill of the chase is what it's all about.

risk at the hands of another road user. But there are ways to go beyond that, to go one better, heck, to go six better. You can be the motorcyclist your coworkers know. You can be the motorcyclist your friends know. You can be the motorcyclist your relatives know. You can be the motorcyclist your spouse knows. And you can be the motorcyclist that other motorcyclists know—not other riders, but by taking those people who don't ride out with you on the back of your bike, you make them motorcyclists for a while. Show them firsthand what it's all about. Show them how much fun it is, how human it is, give them a little bit of the joy that you feel when you ride, and they will take it with them and use that memory when they're on the road with other motorcyclists.

Play Your Position

I had a college instructor who told me in no uncertain terms that if a kid throws a snowball and it hits my car, it was my patriotic duty as an adult to slam on the brakes, whip the car onto the shoulder or into a driveway, get out, roar like an angry lion, and then chase that kid for all I'm worth. What fun is throwing snowballs at cars if they just keep on driving? The near-death experience is what it's all about.

Like the civic duty of chasing down cheeky adolescents with snowballs, you have civic duties as a motorcyclist, too. Your behavior can affect your own future risk and the risks that other motorcyclists face. A good deed might be noticed and rewarded. It may not be you who's rewarded, and it may not be right that moment, but maybe to someone somewhere down the road. A bad deed might also get noticed and the favor returned, maybe now, maybe later. The net long-term effect is what we're looking for here, not the immediate result. It's an important consideration.

What can you do to make friends in your neighborhood and maybe reduce your risk there? Of course, you can start by being smart about noise. While a quiet motorcyclist probably won't get much attention, a noisy one definitely will—and bad attention, at that. Acting conscientious of noise from the exhaust pipe, especially during the quiet hours, probably won't earn you too many friend points, but it probably also won't cost you any. Remember, when your house is the staging area for a Sunday-morning group ride, that your riding friends must also understand that you live in a quiet neighborhood and they need to respect other people's sleep time.

Another civic duty done for the benefit of motorcycle riders everywhere. I can just hear the dinner conversation later, "Mom, how old do you have to be to ride a motorcycle?"

A rider can also deliberately minimize his or her outward displays while riding in their own neighborhood or any residential area. Harsh and loud acceleration, riding fast, and bouncing over curbs might be legal, but might also look obnoxious to the nonrider. You can help keep your upstanding reputation and maybe add to motorcyclists' reputation by behaving in an extracautious manner around people's homes. Try riding around at 20 or 25 instead of the posted 30. Corner carefully, looking well ahead to who might be playing in the street or mowing their lawn or working on their P.O.S. beater car and give them plenty of extra room, exaggerating it for emphasis.

When mounting your driveway, make a real show out of slowing carefully, approaching at a right angle, pointing the bike up toward the garage, then gently easing the tires, first front, then back, over the curb. Not only can a show like this prove how careful you are, but it could also hint to someone that maybe motorcycles need a little extra attention when it comes to bumps in the road. Maybe riders need to be really careful with stuff that cars only scoff at. Make other people think, "Maybe, in general, I should just give riders more room and allow them to get around as safely as they can. They have to balance those things, they're probably a lot more work to ride than my car is to drive."

Scoring Points for the Good Guys

Making a point of smiling and waving at people who live near you can take some of the mystery out of who you are, and maybe they'll come to associate a friendly neighbor with a motorcycle. Then when they see a motorcycle that looks like yours, they might think to themselves, "So-and-so down the street rides a bike like that. I better give him some more room just in case it's him. I don't want to piss off my *neighbor*." Riding down the slippery slope, maybe your neighbor will come to associate all motorcycles with you and your friendly, careful, conscientious ways and give them all the room and respect they need and deserve.

You can take this sort of approach to public relations to work with you, too. Making friends in the neighborhood is easy, but at work, people don't know as much about you. They're not supposed to know as much about you. They might not know what you drive, they might not know how well you take care of your yard, they might not know that your kids play with their kids. You're just the person in engineering who they have to deal with when they have a problem. Here in the office, it's important to take steps to make friends.

"Should I cut this guy off? Do I know this guy? Is that my neighbor? Better not risk it. . . ." One point for the home team.

Make a habit of smiling and waving to people who live near you to take some of the mystery out of who you are. Maybe they'll come to associate a friendly neighbor with a motorcycle and treat other motorcyclists better because of it.

Go ahead. Be corny. Schmooze. Be a big, happy teddy bear. When someone will identify you as a motorcyclist, the impression you make could affect other motorcyclists in the future. Be approachable, be easy to read, and always, always be friendly. You're reducing the risk of those people taking a rider's safety or rights for granted someday.

Ride extra respectfully in the company parking lot or ramp, just as you do in your neighborhood. If the sign says 20, do 10. Ride exaggeratedly deliberate and park carefully in designated areas. Be especially mindful when riding up the sidewalk to park by the building or taking a little corner somewhere that isn't actually a parking spot. Some people might not understand why you park in anything other than an 8-foot-wide parking stall. Some people might not understand why you ride your bike where they're trying to walk. Scattering pedestrians willy-nilly to reach your special spot quicker is a *bad* idea. Wait patiently, smiling, until your path is completely clear and then carefully, cautiously, slide your bike into place.

When someone gives you that look that says, "Why is that motorcycle rider so important that they get to park on the sidewalk?" make it a point to tell them how great it is that the company allows you to park in unused areas in order to make more room for everyone else. Tell them, "It sure makes it easier to park right up by the building, because bikes are a lot easier to steal or tip over when they're out of sight. We work for a really great company that appreciates how motorcycles help with congestion and parking. Plus, I'm always happier and more productive at work when I get to ride in the morning." Go ahead. Be a ham. Be a big, friendly teddy bear. Whenever anyone can identify you as a motorcyclist, be approachable, be easy to read, and always, always be friendly. You're reducing the risk of those people taking a rider's safety or rights for granted someday.

You can reap benefits of making friends anywhere. Try it on the road. While it's not so common anymore to drive courteously, there are still a lot of people who do. And there are even more people still out there who *expect* others to do so. Don't be that one person that day that ticked them off.

No, you don't have to turn into a complete sap, letting people drive all over you by constantly giving up your right of way. No, sir. (Well, I mean, you can if you want, but doing it indiscriminately and all the time might not make you any friends. That might actually send the wrong message, the one that suggests motorcyclists are supposed to allow other drivers to have the right of way.) No, the trick to this is to make a spectacle of it, to do it as a *favor* for someone you don't know, just out of the goodness of your heart. Be the one person in a whole crowd of anonymous people who stood out that day by doing something nice.

When pulling up to stopped traffic, leave extra room in front of you and wave someone out of a parking space. Wave them out with a smile. Motion harried commuters into traffic by slowing and allowing them room—especially when others won't. You have to make sure that if you're going to expend the effort, you do it when you'll get the most friend points possible. Making room for someone on an on ramp will only win you points if someone sees you making room.

An important note about courtesy on the road: Give it a touch of Hollywood. Remember that ridiculous movie where the meteors exploded in huge fireballs on impact instead of just hitting the ground like the big rocks that they were? No one will remember a smooth transition made by a motorcyclist from one lane to the other just to make room for a merging vehicle.

What will they remember? They'll remember a motorcyclist whose eyes widened and looked suddenly surprised (and who seemed to be in great danger) by the appearance of the merging vehicle. They'll remember the rider's head turning sharply, the rider's eyes finding theirs and making direct contact, then a nod, "Okay, I see, you need to get in here and I'm in your way." They'll remember the rider's head swiveling around quickly to check traffic on the other side, glancing at the mirror, doing a headcheck, then mirror again, then headcheck again, then making a great show of signaling and moving over, or slowing down, or speeding up, to allow room for the merger. Use a great big hand signal as well as your turn signal. Make a big production out of it. Without taking any unnecessary risks, make it look as if you're really going out of your way for someone. They'll remember.

To make friends for motorcyclists where it's really important, try an old political trick. When you're out in wonderful rural America, fill your tank when it's only half empty. Stop for gas, a break, and a snack

If a motorcyclist does a good deed and no one is around to see it, is it still a good deed? Of course. But make sure you also do it when people are watching—even if you have to wait for someone to walk by. And exaggerate it.

even when you don't really need to. If you can, stop only at the little podunk places out in the middle of nowhere, rather than the big chain gas stations in the larger towns. Top off your tank, B.S. with the owner for a few minutes, stick a couple quarters into the soda machine, tell a joke. Guys in the boondocks are usually looking to chat and really need and appreciate your business. If you teach those people that motorcyclists are good customers and fun to talk to, you've scored another point for the good guys.

So we've covered home, work, and the road, but is there anywhere else? Sure, there's everywhere else. But you need to be creative, and you need to make a show of it. Anytime you can be obviously identified as a motorcyclist, turn into the role-model Boy Scout. Help old ladies across the street. Get stranded cats from trees. Rescue little Timmy from the bottom of the well. You get the idea.

Before You Hit the Road:
- Make friends in the neighborhood.
- Make friends at work.
- Make friends in public.
- Every meeting is an opportunity to score points for the food guys. Use it.

Great Idea #777: Don't stop for gas when you need to, stop when you want to—and never use more than half a tank if you have the time. Stop, top it off, B.S. with the owner for a few minutes, buy a bag of peanuts, get a cold drink from the machine, ask about the weather or construction or some dumb thing. Filling station owners in deep rural America are good talkers. They appreciate the money and time you spend there much more than the high-school-aged clerk at the mega-truck-plaza-convenience-store chain station. You want the guy at the station to look forward to seeing motorcycle riders on the horizon.

TROUBLE AREAS

When situations change, the risks increase. When things change abruptly, things get risky. Trouble areas are those in which it is very common for the layout, traffic, mindset, and environment to automatically change, thus changing the level of risk the rider faces.

Smoothly flowing traffic carries with it a minor level of risk. Drivers get into the groove and generally try to do what everyone else is doing. But when changes in the roadway itself—intersections, merge areas, lane shifts—change the flow of traffic, more personal judgment and decision making come into play. Just as two different people will have entirely different hairstyles or clothing, two motorists aiming for the same lane may have entirely different ideas about when to move there, how to alert others to their intentions, at what speed to perform the maneuver, and who has the right of way. The flow of traffic changes, sometimes dramatically, due to the differences in opinion of how things should be done. The big trouble areas are the ones where these differences are inevitable or the layout of the road and the mindset of the populace make conflict unavoidable.

You can know in advance what you're going to be dealing with around the next corner. Choose when you can, but otherwise, be prepared.

Rush Hours

Crashes and injuries spike during the morning and afternoon rush hours. This shouldn't come as a surprise. There are more road users clogging the asphalt arteries during rush hour. Everybody's out there at once, trying to get to where they need to be to pay the bills. More people using the roads—including pedestrians and bicyclists—mean more distractions and more ways for the surroundings to encroach upon attention. More traffic means less breathing room, fewer escape routes, and fewer options for planning your path of travel. More road users mean more blind spots in which to accidentally find yourself.

They're all in various states of readiness. In the morning, they're half asleep, listening to the radio, drinking scalding hot liquids, or eating messy fast food. In the afternoon, they're either pumped up or tuckered out from a day at work, they're distracted by either what they've just finished or what they're about to begin, and they're probably a little sweatier, a little dirtier, and a little greasier than they were eight hours before.

The need to be someplace at a certain time brings out drivers who feel the need to hurry, which is a bad idea in *any* vehicle. If you want to go fast, by all means, go fast. But don't put the cart before the horse. Hurrying makes the destination the priority and not the trip, and when a person stops thinking about where they are in favor of where they desperately feel they need to be, mistakes get made. Accidents happen. Don't ever, ever hurry on a motorcycle. If you feel the need, you shouldn't be in the saddle or behind the wheel of anything. Hurrying is like giving up your mental strategy to focus on "getting there." Hurrying essentially bumps you up one complete risk level.

Risk goes up for all these reasons. If you have the option, considering traveling at another time or using a different route to avoid the problems that go along with congestion.

Intersections

You can't change the fact that intersections are the most dangerous places for motorcyclists. So if you want to lower your risk in intersections, one way to do so is to choose the intersections you need to traverse more carefully. Here you have an opportunity to make a decision for a reason and not because of habit. Remember that three right turns equal one left turn, and there are often many more ways than one to arrive at a destination.

Let's pretend that you need to turn 10 times to get from home to work every day. Would a route involving all left turns be safer, or less safe, than a route involving only right turns? Would a route featuring a stop sign at every turn be safer, or less safe, than a route featuring stoplights? What about a route without any controls at all? You can control the types of situations you put yourself into by choosing a route that avoids big breaks in the flow of traffic or one that incorporates breaks in the flow that are not as dramatic.

Think hard about your route. Where and when you change directions is almost completely up to you. Turn where it's safest. We know all about intersections and how risky they are for motorcyclists. But different intersections have different levels of risk, and different approaches to an intersection have different levels of risk. Ask yourself these questions:

• Which type of traffic control at a four-way intersection is most risky, a traffic signal, a four-way stop, or a two-way stop?

• Which type of turn at these intersections, a right or a left, is more risky?

• Which is more risky, turning with the sun behind you or looking into it?

It's not a big leap to guess that the time period in which a traffic light is yellow is a dangerous time for a motorcycle rider, especially in heavy traffic. Yellow lights are usually a surprise to most drivers, and the vicious amber light brings out the impulse decision maker in all of us. The motorcyclist must make a split-second decision whether to go or slow. The woman on the cell phone in the enormous sport-utility vehicle tailgating you must also make the same decision. If they make

Don't ever, ever hurry on a motorcycle. What you may gain in time saved or meetings promptly attended doesn't even compare to what you give up in attention and concentration skills. If you have to be somewhere in a hurry, get someone else to drive or take the time to relax and be late on purpose.

Think hard about your route. Where and when you change directions is almost completely up to you. Turn where it's safest.

99

The Dreaded Yellow: You can choose whether or not to deal with the yellow light to some degree. If you know the light will change before you get there, you can begin slowing down or braking early to force tailgaters or other poor decision makers to either slow down or go around you. Or you can speed up to put some distance between you and those behind you, although this cuts the distance between you and those in front of you and also increases your stopping time and distance. While it's not a perfect science, it is possible to time your arrival at intersections.

Would you rather turn left here . . .

. . . or right here . . .

. . .and then left here? The right-and-then-left turn gets you to your destination about five seconds later than the left turn. How badly do you want to save time? Or put another way, how badly do you want to decrease your risk? Sometimes three right turns equal a left turn.

completely different decisions, it could be very good or very bad for the rider. The vehicles in the oncoming lane trying to turn across your path of travel need to make the same decision, also. The cars in the cross traffic, waiting to turn right are in the process of making the same decision. Simply put, the yellow light represents the worst time to be in the most dangerous place for a motorcycle—in an intersection.

There are tips elsewhere in this book for dealing with the whole question of "go or no go," and using your mind and body to position yourself in time and space (and mindset) to minimize your risk in these situations. But it's also important to remember that you can choose whether or not to deal with the yellow light to some degree. If you know the light will change before you get to it, you can begin slowing down or braking early, even before the light changes, to force tailgaters or other poor decision makers to either slow or go around you. You can speed up to put some distance between you and those behind you, although this cuts the distance between you and those in front of you and also increases your stopping time and distance. While it's not a perfect science, it is possible to time your arrival at intersections to avoid the dreaded yellow.

Intersections are tough enough when you know about them in advance. What about those times when you're surprised by one? There are usually some indicators that can give you an advance warning:

• Look for breaks in the scenery. A gap in the trees could mean a side road or driveway.
• Watch the signs. Most roads have one or more signs leading up to the intersection.
• Watch the pavement. Black skid marks on your side or muddy tractor-tire tracks on the other side can spell trouble.

Rural Roads

Rural roads can be the best and the worst places to ride. But the relative beauty and lack of traffic can lull you into a foolhardy

sense of safety, so beware of sleeping with your eyes open. You still need to plan ahead and expect things like gravel, boulders, and rocks strewn all throughout a blind corner. You need to prepare for lazy drivers who are used to the fact that no one really watches what they do out there, farm implements with no other choice but to use the road, muddy tire tracks, friendly and frightened and foolhardy animals, and trees, lots of trees. Big, leafy, dark, woodsy trees just love to hide tricky corners and

Would you rather take this road . . .

. . . and turn here . . .

. . . or take this road . . .

. . . and turn here? One takes a little longer than the other, but is the added risk of the shorter road worth the time saved? Sure, you sacrifice some economy of route, but you gain economy of safety.

Ah, decisions. While you hope that this driver is deciding whether it's safer to pull out or to wait for the light to turn green, he is really trying to decide whether to eat his fries or his double thumperburger first.

101

The best rural roads inspire many riders to go faster than they should. Beauty begets beauty, and there's nothing more thrilling than working a bike over to the tune of summer sun, wild flowers, fresh air, and farmhouses. But remember that the speed differential is greatest on rural roads, 55 miles per hour or more as the fastest speed, 1 mile per hour as the slowest.

Beware: Suburban predictability brings out the worst in people who have no choice but to suffer through it every day. Drivers who commute through suburban areas every day often learn the timing of the lights and the flow of the traffic but not much else.

More frustrating than city streets and urban superslabs combined, suburban traffic can be the most dangerous because of high speeds and high speed differentials.

driveways that rarely move out of the way when you accidentally venture off-highway. And you need to expect the completely unexpected. A friend of mine once slid in a giant puddle of milk while riding in rural Wisconsin, giving knew meaning to that state's status as America's "Dairyland."

The best rural roads inspire many riders to go faster than they should. Remember that the speed differential is greatest on rural roads, 55 miles per hour or more as the fastest speed, 1 mile per hour as the slowest. If you're sightseeing, slow down and see the sights. Keep your speed to a level that allows you to divert attention to things other than the road. If you're sport riding, keep your speeds legal in the straights and save your frisky business for the corners. A mistake at high speed can be deadly in the backwoods, while a mistake in a 30-miles-per-hour corner might not be so dramatic. However, keep an eye out and watch carefully to know where you are. Some 30-miles-per-hour corners end in cornfields and others in ravines.

Suburbs

Suburban roads can be the most dangerous, especially for riders who are too familiar and comfortable with the patterns. Drivers who commute through suburban areas

every day learn the timing of the lights and the flow of the traffic. If everyone were analytical about it, traffic would probably flow smoothly and with few surprises. Unfortunately, drivers take the opportunity to instead be lazy. They eat, drink, make up their faces, talk business, read, and generally conduct other business in the down time between stoplights. Beware: Suburban predictability brings out the worst in people who have no choice but to suffer through it every day.

While not as great as on rural roads, the speed differential in the suburbs and exurbs is still stupefying, even more so if you take into account the possibly asinine expectation that road users will be going slower than on a rural highway. It's not unusual to see speeds of 60 or 70 miles per hour when 45 or 50 is posted. Combine such speeds with a vehicle lurching forward from a stop into traffic and you've got rural differentials with the consequences of freeways.

In addition to a large speed differential, suburban arterials have a great deal of action to contend with: neighborhoods bordering four-lane roads; high-school kids with their own cars; restaurants of the fast-food and not-so-fast-food varieties; soccer moms; yellow lights; turn lanes; painted

City streets seem to have the closest quarters, but a keen and unconventional eye can find escape routes that don't exist for other motorists. Pat Hahn

Choosing a six-lane slab over a city street reduces your risk of a crash but increases your risk of death and dismemberment.

Put it this way: City drivers either have somewhere to be and are timing it to the minute, or they're completely lost and about to cause a crash, or at least tick off someone else. Both types are high risk to a city rider, but for different reasons.

included in this subject, but city driving has a few idiosyncrasies that need extra attention.

The various distractions of city riding—clustered buildings, buses, varieties of road surfaces, bicycles, pedestrians, parallel parking, alleys, hidden entrances, and clogged traffic—make it the most chancy place to ride. Most of the road users in the city are people who use them every day, know the route, and have a pretty comfortable familiarity with the lanes, lights, and turns, but the rest are people who have never been there before and are therefore completely bewildered and very unpredictable. Put it this way: They either have somewhere to be and are timing it to the minute, or they're completely lost. Those who are lost are the ones who are going to clog traffic and cause a crash because of people trying to get around them. And just like the suburbs, drivers who are too familiar with a pattern can cause trouble because they

Keep an eye out for someone driving really slowly—they may cause a problem for someone in the very near future. And get used to the idea that you may need to split lanes, jump off your bike, or drive up on the sidewalk to avoid a crash.

lines; distractions like marquis slogans, pedestrians, and bicyclists; and people generally in the really big hurry.

City Streets

Here's where you're most likely to have a crash but least likely to become a fatality. This really goes for any and all of a metropolitan area where speeds are generally slower and road users more numerous than on rural roads and freeways, metropolitan or otherwise. To be truthful, suburban and exurban areas should be

Only two hours difference between maximum density and reasonable breathing room. If you can, adjust your schedule to travel during the lower-risk times.

become less alert to others and more focused on following a certain series of steps.

Combine the all-or-nothing familiarity level of other drivers with the facts that riders simply have less breathing room, fewer clear escape routes, and lots of blind-spot dwellers, and you've got a recipe for a sure-fire low-speed crash. In heavy traffic like that, it's inevitable. Beware of becoming too used to a route. Vary it from time to time to keep alert. Keep an eye out for people with their blinkers on for a long time or people driving really slowly—they may cause problems for those behind them in the very near future. Get used to the idea that you may need to split lanes or drive on the sidewalk to avoid a crash. Practice this, visualize it, and go through the motions when you can do so safely. And don't let yourself get distracted by pedestrians and window dressing. One moment of inattention can cost a lot.

Freeways

The big roads with controlled access, high speeds, and predictable behavior are the exact opposite of city streets. Choosing a six-lane slab over a city street reduces your risk of a crash but increases your risk of death and dismemberment. Higher speeds

lead to higher rates of injury and fatality, remember? Mistakes on the freeways are likely to be far more dramatic than those on slower roads. On the other hand, slower roads will give you less likelihood of death and injury but more likelihood of a crash. It's a tradeoff that you have to make. With which consequence are you more comfortable? In which situation do you feel more in control? There's no right or wrong, only what's right or wrong for you.

The two primary problems with freeways fortunately occur separately most of the time. Each has its own unique flavor and both have the same easy solutions. Both also have more difficult different solutions. Maybe you'll like them, maybe you won't.

The first is the heavy-traffic, rush-hour, city-dweller variety. Even though the road size doesn't change, drivers somehow manage to squeeze several times as many vehicles onto the same roadway as during low-volume times or rural freeways of the same size. Space cushions and following distances all disappear without anyone even realizing it. Drivers maintain the same cushions and distance at 60 miles per hour as they do at 30, when they have to. They're using slow-speed driving techniques in high-speed situations. With the unpredictability (or is it?) of stop-and-go

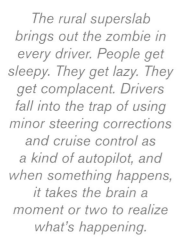

Zinging through a cloverleaf following another vehicle too closely is a sure-fire way to test your braking-in-a-curve skills. Any judge who saw you would say, "You were asking for it."

traffic, the rear-end crashes of the type that Mr. Hurt promised us only happen three percent of the time are far more likely. So as a motorcyclist, you are stuck in the unsavory position of as many potential hazards as in the city but at greatly increased speed and risk levels.

The other major risk factor associated with freeways is the sleeping driver. Once outside the metro areas, life on the freeways becomes *very* predictable. There's plenty of room to accommodate merging vehicles, sight lines are generally good, the drone of the pavement underneath is relaxing, and there's more time to do important stuff like fiddle with the radio, read the newspaper, or eat heavily salted snack treats or fast food. Finally, some time to relax, right? Yikes.

The slab brings out the worst in everybody. People get sleepy. People get lazy. People get complacent. Drivers get into the zone of making minor steering corrections and using cruise control, and when something happens, it takes their brains a moment or two to realize what's happening. Many times, by then, it's too late. Moving at 88 feet per second, a lot can happen when two heavy objects collide.

You know what I'm going to tell you already. The best way to avoid these bad

situations is to not be there in the first place. If you have to face a commute home in heavy traffic, take the side roads and skip the freeway. If you have to face a long, boring superslab trek across several states, again, take the side roads and skip the freeway. The attributes of each bring out the worst in both drivers and motorcycle riders. Sure, the side roads will take you longer, but they're more interesting anyway. The difference in summer construction holdups alone is worth the extra time on the road.

If you choose to use the freeway, there are a couple things to remember that can help lower your risk. There are usually decent shoulders on the road that make good escape routes when you need them. There is also usually a decent amount of room between lanes to use if you need it. The big breaks in the flow are usually fairly predictable.

People who learned to drive on a different planet don't know that the left lane is for passing. Expect them to pile traffic up behind them and for people to risk your life trying to get around the parade. Also expect last-minute dashes for exit ramps, and pay close attention when you're in the middle or right lane and an exit's approaching. Also anticipate that one-in-a-thousand

"The Keepers of the Speed," people who learned to drive on Mars or Jupiter, don't know that the left lane is for passing, so don't be surprised when they cause problems. Expect them to pile traffic up behind them and for people to risk your life trying to get around the parade.

Expect last-minute dashes for exit ramps, and pay close attention when you're in the middle or right lane and an exit's approaching.

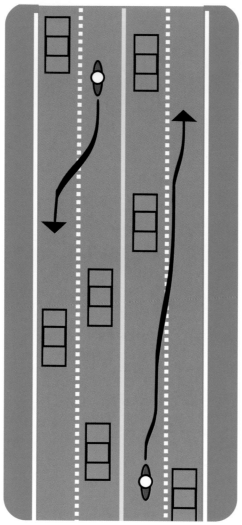

The oncoming rider is making a normal lane change, one movement, position A to position B. It's adequate, but it could be made safer by a soft lane change. The rider at bottom is changing lanes softly, starting at point A, encroaching on the centerline, holding position, then crossing over and encroaching on the other lane, then holding position, then moving to point B.

The Art of the Soft Lane Change

The most death-defying feats performed by motorcyclists today are those that involve heavy traffic, particularly on freeways where the speeds are high and the consequences of mistakes even higher. The soft lane change has saved my life and is a simple and powerful inclusion into any riding strategy, any time and anywhere. Let me first tell you the story.

Riding back to Minneapolis from Michigan City, my unfortunate choice was I-94 through Chicago to Milwaukee. Posted 55, the traffic on that Sunday morning whipped along at a modest 75 with very little variation in speed from vehicle to vehicle.

In Chicagoland, however, packs of young, aggressive drivers frequently move at 15 to 30 miles per hour faster than the rest of the traffic. This appears to be some sort of race and involves a half-dozen or more cars weaving, swerving, braking, and passing the slower traffic in a hurry to get to the next toll booth or fast-food joint or wherever they're going.

As I said, I was in the middle lane of the three-lane freeway and literally practicing and honing the technique of the soft lane change, which I had only just discovered. I was surprised by a blue-and-white Dodge Ram pickup—you know, the one with the big stripes up the center to make it look like a race car. The driver passed me on the left going about 100. I was surprised, but not alarmed. I only became alarmed when a half-second later, a Mustang GT also passed me on the left at what must have been more like 110, cut in front of me and then blew past the Dodge and then back to the left lane. Yikes!

I signaled, quickly checked my right-hand mirror and blind spot, and moved *softly* into the right lane, thinking there may be more. Just as I crossed the dashed white line to my right, a red Pontiac Grand Am or Grand Prix or some other poor man's race car roared by my right elbow, its draft pulling me forward and to the right, causing me to nearly swing in behind it as it cleared my front tire. The driver had to be going at least 100 while I was still hanging at 75. Young Richard Rasierre (Ricky Racer) came within about four feet of my

hyper-cautious driver who slams on the brakes with both feet at the bottom of entrance ramps. Know the location of common speed traps and slowdown areas and prepare ahead of time for the brake lights. And when you're in a situation where you cannot see well, remember which vehicles have a great line of sight and also need the most room to stop— tractor-trailers—and follow their lead. Aside from sports-car enthusiasts, professional drivers are the only other ones out there who really seem to care about driving, flow, and etiquette.

right mirror, then swerved hard left and back across the center lane and into the far left lane. Immediately afterward, about six more vehicles passed me at well over 90 in the left and middle lanes, weaving in and out of traffic, all chasing the leader in the Mustang. It was lucky for me that that kid had good 18-year-old reflexes.

What saved me that day was the soft lane change.

The purpose of this technique is to allow yourself and other road users time and space to make mistakes. This is realism, folks. Everybody makes mistakes so why not allow for them rather than suffer from them? You can actually create time and space where there was none before, just as banks, through loans, create money that did not exist until you signed the paperwork. On any road, traveling any direction, and making any maneuver, changing lanes softly rather than hard is a risk-reduction technique that does its job every single time, no matter where, no matter when. It is especially useful on busy freeways and in busy urban traffic situations where things happen fast and drivers change lanes and position often, cutting through traffic to reach an exit or zig-zagging along trying to beat everyone to the next stoplight. The soft lane change allows you to pick a different position or direction while allowing the most margin for error in judgment, whether that error is yours or theirs.

Here's how it works: When you move from one lane to another, after you've checked your blind spot carefully and your mirror thoroughly, flash your turn signal and move over. But instead of sliding smoothly from the center of the old lane to the center of the new lane, move quickly but just barely across the line that divides the two lanes, and then hold that position, leaving your turn signal on. Wait a moment for a honk or some other indicator that you've missed some important information. After a couple seconds, if you hear or see no problems, smoothly and deliberately adjust your position to the area of the new lane you prefer. Once you've reached your new path of travel, then turn off the blinker. Basically, you're turning what was one motion into two, giving others an additional chance to

make room for you. When it's life or death, I'd always choose a second chance, wouldn't you?

The degree of "softness" has everything to do with the amount of room available. If the opposite side of the lane into which you're moving has a large shoulder, obviously you have a lot of room to work with. If it only has a limited amount of space, such as on a bridge or against a jersey barrier, you have very little room to work with. Think of the space that you leave open and the room left available beyond that as the runout. In case of a mistake, this is the other driver's obvious or default path of travel. If it has only a thin strip of concrete or asphalt, the amount of space you initially take up in the new lane should be no more than the width of the shoulder area—that way, even after making a lane change, you still leave, in theory, an entire lane for someone else to work with if they need to.

Making your lane change precisely, but softly and gradually, leaves a tremendous amount of room for error. In my case on I-94 that day, when I moved from the center lane to the right lane, by initially holding my position just to the right of the centerline, I left nearly the entire right lane plus the equally wide shoulder for that stupid little moron in the Pontiac. Both of our paths of travel converged in that one point in time and space, but because of the soft shift, we could share it for a moment rather than flipping a coin for it. (In a coin toss between a car and a bike trying to share space, the bike never, ever wins.) My mistake was that I didn't expect a right-hand lane change problem to come from my left side. The other driver must have come from the far left lane and tried to pass me on the right by swerving over two lanes.

My effort at leaving room for someone who may need it worked, and the problem vehicle only had to move over a couple more feet, rather than an entire lane (and onto the shoulder). If I had moved directly to the raised oil-slick area or the right-hand portion, I probably would have been rear-ended at 75 miles per hour in heavy traffic. The consequences would have been severe.

By using this technique every time, if

Making your lane change precisely, but softly and gradually, leaves a tremendous amount of room for error.

Lifesaving Tip: When in doubt, slow it down.

Thinking back to Chapter 4, remember that with higher speed, a rider faces more risks. With lower speed, a rider faces fewer risks—especially when it comes to an unanticipated dismount or multivehicle crash. There is almost no hazard or hazardous situation in which a rider cannot lower the risk by reducing speed. (Tailgaters and impending rear-end collisions are notable exceptions.)

Your immediate, instinctive, automatic response to any unknown or untried hazard (as opposed to the known or visualized, as in the preceding chapter), should always be to get your speed down. This reduces the rate at which the hazard approaches and effectively buys you time and space to plan your next move.

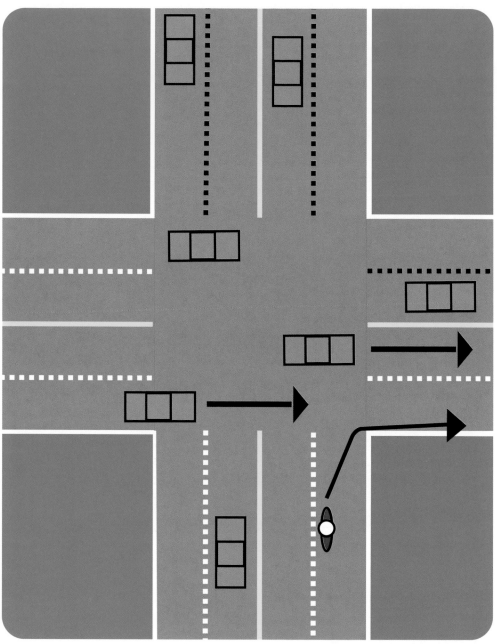

Turning softly is another way to reduce your risk. Instead of barging into traffic because you believe your lane is clear, claim road space gently at first, in case you missed something or someone changes lanes at the last minute.

you overlook a vehicle in your blind spot and move over, you've only just barely encroached in their road space, and both you and the other person have the time and space to make up for it. You can speed up or move back over to your original lane if you need to. The other driver can back off or change lanes or speed up and get around you with space to spare.

Another example would be the situation in which the car directly behind you

decides to change lanes at the same time and sharks you into the next lane. By changing position softly, you've still left nearly an entire lane to make up for the mistake and the time in which to do it. By contrast, if you accidentally ignored a vehicle in your blind spot or one in the next lane moving quite a bit faster than you, and you quickly change positions from the center of one lane to the center of another, you've cut off that other person's path of travel and his or her simplest escape route at the same time. That's not leaving yourself much room!

You can use this technique absolutely anywhere. When making any kind of turn, instead of immediately proceeding to your favorite position in the lane, hug the closest edge of the lane for a few seconds to allow other people to get used to you being there. A vehicle you missed, or one that changed lanes after you last looked, will still have room to get around you, rather than running into the back of your bike and adding you to the collection of mangled riders in the hospital. Or morgue.

We all make mistakes, and battling urban traffic is always a mixture of riding smart and understanding the habits and weaknesses of traffic, including your own. Using the soft lane change creates a new and larger margin for error, allows you and other drivers to make sudden adjustments at a more manageable pace, and can make changing position or direction on any roadway less of a life-or-death situation.

Shadowing

Let's look at risk from a different point of view. If you were in a car and you had to pull out in front of someone, who would it be?

Picture yourself sitting at a stop sign. You're trying to cross a divided four-lane highway. The traffic is heavy, and it's rush hour, so everyone's in a hurry. You've got to get across, but there are no safe openings.

The traffic is rural highway, with lots of big cars, pickup trucks, and 18-wheelers. To pull out in front of any of them would

be suicide. But wait—there's an opening—right after that white minivan. You decide to make a run for it, but just as the minivan passes and you lurch out into traffic, you realize there's a motorcycle there that you completely missed. But now it's too late. You're committed, and you've just taken the life of yet another motorcyclist.

Or try this: picture yourself at the same stop sign. You're still trying to get across the highway and the traffic's not so heavy, but this time, the sun is in your eyes—you can't see anything except silhouettes. You wait and wait and wait, squinting into the blinding sun, your hand over your eyes, and then you see an opening—no silhouettes! You gun the throttle and surge forward without realizing there's a motorcycle right there. There, you killed another one.

Or how about this one: same intersection, same plan. (Question: Why did the motorist cross the road? Answer: To get to the other side.) This time, the traffic's heavy *and* the sun's blinding you, but that doesn't matter. Your deal is that you just don't give a whit. You're going to pull out and let everybody *else* get out of *your* way. But you're not stupid. You're not going to just pull out in front of a great big semi. You'll wait until you see a vehicle that's a little smaller. One that can stop fast. Ahhh . . . there's one!

It really doesn't matter why. People pull out in front of motorcycles all the time. It's seldom the motorcyclist's fault, but it's always the rider's problem. Bikes are hard

When making any kind of turn, instead of immediately proceeding to your favorite position in the lane, hug the closest edge of the lane for a few seconds to allow other people to get used to you being there.

Don't ever assume they see you. Ever.

109

An example of shadowing: Keep mental notes on the intersections in which you can use another vehicle to run interference for you. Keeping a large vehicle nearby as you ride, or riding from large vehicle to large vehicle, works too.

When approaching an intersection with cars waiting to cross or waiting to turn, ride in the "shadow" of a car or truck.

to see and don't pose much of a threat in a collision. It's inevitable. But there is a way to protect yourself.

When approaching an intersection with cars waiting to cross or waiting to turn, ride in the "shadow" of a car or truck. Sure, you may blend in with that vehicle and be harder to see, but most people would be less likely to pull out in front of a bus, right? Even if you have to ride in the other driver's blind spot for a few seconds, you've put yourself into a better position to deal with the biggest hazard—someone violating your right of way and your path of travel. The risk you avoid is worth the risk you take. Once you've cleared the intersection, you then speed up or back off from the vehicle you were shadowing.

The Technique
Ride in the center of your lane just next to the vehicle you're shadowing. If your biggest hazard will come from the left side, ride on the left side of the vehicle. If your biggest hazard will come from the right side, ride on the right side of the vehicle. If you don't have a choice, then you don't have a choice—ride on whichever side you can. Your back tire should be even with the rear bumper of the vehicle you're shadowing. While this is not ordinarily a safe place to be, it is the safest place to be for this

technique. This position allows you to keep a close eye on your greatest potential hazards. It also allows you the ability to brake quickly to clear out of the blind spot you're sitting in if the other driver decides to change lanes and doesn't see you. (For these reasons, it's a bad idea to shadow a vehicle in the area of its front bumper.)

If hazards are approaching from *both* sides, you may be safest to tailgate the vehicle you're shadowing—at a safe distance as you approach the intersection (so you can see ahead to either side and to give others the opportunity to see you) and then quickly close the distance and ride right on the rear bumper while passing *through* the intersection. This presents its own danger (tailgating another vehicle that may have to stop quickly) but if you're aware of that danger and your skills are up to par, you can probably stop faster than a bus, anyway. But the few seconds you put yourself in danger may far outweigh the risks you're avoiding.

Either way, once past the hazard, you need to immediately back off or speed up and find another safe position. If you're going to be dealing with the same types of hazards over and over again on the same stretch of road, it may be wise to back off and keep the larger vehicle nearby so you can shadow it again.

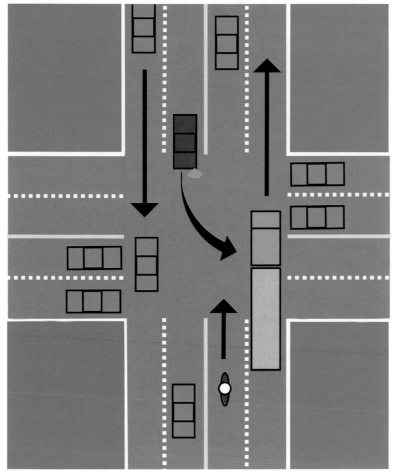

Your back tire should be even with the rear bumper of the vehicle. This position allows you to keep a close eye on any left-turning vehicles. It also allows you to brake quickly if you need to.

This technique works in the city, in the suburbs, and out in the country. While intersections are obvious trouble areas, here are some other hints for where to shadow a vehicle:
- Amusement parks
- Beaches
- Car dealerships
- Churches on Sunday
- Closing time
- Dawn and dusk
- Factory parking lots
- Fast-food joints and convenience stores
- High schools
- Hockey rinks
- Movie theaters
- Park and rides
- Pharmacies
- Signs announcing county roads or state highway intersections
- Soccer fields
- Swimming pools
- Yellow lights

If you're approaching any of these trouble spots and you *don't* have a vehicle to shadow, you need to use great care. Just being aware that you're out there on your own and particularly vulnerable is half the battle. Choosing the lane position that makes you most conspicuous, reducing your speed, and covering your brakes and clutch will also greatly lower your risks. Draw attention to yourself, if you have to. Stay alert.

Before You Hit the Road
- Choose your route carefully.
- Don't get too comfortable.
- Change lanes softly.
- When in doubt, slow it down.
- Shadow other vehicles in high-risk intersections.

Just being aware that you're out there on your own and particularly vulnerable is half the battle.

chapter 11

THE WORST TYPES AND YOUR BEST DEFENSE

Some factors are beyond your control, but to know what those uncontrollable factors are can help you avoid them altogether. If you use the three degrees, your biggest risk is probably the other guy. Some other guys are worse than other other guys, or at least more predictably high-risk. Being able to identify them easily, or at least classify other vehicles into smaller groups of risk, can help sort the chaff from the bugs and make a better use of your attention, concentration, and time.

Distracted, inexperienced, slow, lazy, and aggressive drivers all cause problems on the road because they're usually doing something very different from everyone else. They're deviants. They come in all shapes and sizes. In a crowd, it would probably be impossible to tell a good driver from a bad driver. Fortunately, on the road they also communicate their deviance nonverbally through their choice of vehicle, driving style, clothing style, choice of passenger or bumper sticker or rearview dangly thing, or through their vehicle maintenance. Knowing who these people are can help you anticipate their next move and give you enough lead time to avoid whatever situation they're about to create.

Some drivers are stream-of-consciousness road users. Their vehicles seem to move without any predictable path of travel or any logical sequence of events. They don't seem to care what anyone else is doing. They're not necessarily distracted, inexperienced, slow, lazy, or aggressive; they just don't seem to recognize the risk of a collision.

Stereotyping

It's not fair to stereotype people, but it can save your life if done with safety in mind.

No matter where you live, there are certain vehicles that are easily identified as trouble. Every state and every country has them. In my own state, they're Volvos of any kind, Hondas, and Probes. Escorts with a local radio station's bumper stickers bookending the rear license plate tend to be trouble too, but for the life of me I can't figure out why. I don't care why, I just know they're trouble, and they get extra attention from me because of it.

You have probably seen them in your own area. Drivers of certain types of vehicles, Volvos in my state in this instance, are stream-of-consciousness drivers. Their vehicles seem to move without any predictable path of travel or any logical sequence of events. What they want, they get. Where they want to be, they go. When they want to go there, they're there, without any outward sign of a sense of the potential consequences of a mistake. Simply, they don't seem to care what anyone else is doing. It only matters what they want to do.

They're not necessarily distracted, inexperienced, slow, lazy, or aggressive; they just don't seem to recognize the risk of a collision. No matter, because they're easy to spot and they get a big space cushion from me. I expect them to change lanes without regard for my position, to slow without regard for those behind them, and to merge without regard for anything. Problem solved.

Aggressive drivers, both men and women, have particular types of cars that they prefer. In my own state, they are males and females in Honda Civics and Preludes. Sometimes they are males in the lower-cost Acuras. Almost all males in Ford Probes are aggressive. In your own area, they probably prefer some other kind of vehicle, but the attitude that goes into their driving is the same.

By aggressive drivers I mean those who like to compete with other vehicles on the road for position. For these people, driving is something of a game to be played and won in traffic. Every vehicle you deal with contains a potentially aggressive driver, but their buying behavior is predictable and can help you manage your risk by knowing what to look for. Take note of the competitors you deal with every day and see if you can find any similarities in their vehicles of choice. If nothing else, this will help you focus on the vehicles around you.

I first discovered this concept many years ago in Minnesota, when a relative confided in me, "Honda drivers are jerks." Being a kid, I took it for truth and went off into the world with the attitude that all Honda drivers were indeed jerks. I knew in my heart that something about it wasn't right, that you just couldn't say that, but I was not yet beyond my teenage years and therefore not too worldly. Many years later, while studying Aristotle in college, I realized what Uncle Max really meant was that "Jerks like to drive Hondas." A subtle but important (and more cogent) distinction. Honda drivers are not jerks, but jerks in my state like to drive them. There are jerks everywhere in the world. Figure out what cars they like to drive, and give them all the space they need. Let other people deal with them.

Rental Vans

A guy in a full moving van is probably midway through one of the worst days he'll have that year. He probably has about a million distractions like shifting furniture, optional insurance, kids and dogs and goldfish, parallel parking, and unfamiliar roads pulling at his concentration. He's also driving a vehicle he's not familiar with. Have mercy on these people, be patient with them, and give them lots of space. They've got everything they own in the back of a truck and are momentarily without a home. They're probably not too interested in the art of driving safely.

Animals, Kids, Bicycles, Emergency Vehicles

I'm can't say that animals, kids, bicyclists, and emergency vehicles don't know the rules. But I can definitely say that some of the most consistent rule breakers around roadways are animals,

A trusted relative once told me that Honda drivers were jerks. I spent the next 10 years disliking Honda drivers (and Acura drivers, too, just for good measure) because they were all jerks. Even when I met nice ones, I figured, "They still probably drive like jerks." It took me until I studied Aristotle in college to realize that Honda drivers weren't jerks, but jerks did like to drive Hondas. It was an important distinction.

Having pity for this guy's situation rather than being irritated at his ineptness is your best bet. He's probably moving, and he's probably having a bad day already. Don't make it any worse, either for him or for the both of you.

When you hear the sirens or see the flashing lights, you're supposed to pull over, right? Even if the emergency vehicle has a clear lane? Even if it's on the other side of a divided highway? Even if you're not even on the same road? Most motorists would say yes to that. They learned in driver's ed class that when you see the flashing lights, you pull over. Lights equal pull over. Take great care to hear and see the siren and lights before everyone else does and adjust your position or get off the road entirely.

kids, bicyclists, and emergency vehicles. Their behavior is easy enough to predict.

Where the problem lies is in the fact that dogs, children, bicyclists, and flashing emergency lights cause many drivers to absolutely lose their minds and forget everything they know about driving. This places those around them in the unsavory position of not only having a true distraction in the rule breaker but also having to deal with nearsighted drivers' snap decision making.

As with everything else, getting your speed down can help reduce the risks posed by these sorts of hazards. During situations when other drivers may risk everyone else's life (or their own) to avoid mangling Cleatus the cocker spaniel, quickly beefing up your space cushion by putting time and distance between you and those closest to the hazard will buy you space to maneuver quickly if you have to. When you're suddenly distracted by a beautiful young hardbody on a bicycle or in-line skates, you need to immediately recognize your distraction as such and assume that the driver behind you is about to plow into your backside in a daze of animal lust.

At those times when you suddenly see or hear a blaring emergency vehicle

approaching, your first priority is to get out of the way of those trying in haste to get out of *its* way. Make sure you're in a position that won't suddenly become home to a frantic SUV driver trying to impress everyone with her knowledge of the rules of the road. She's doing what she believes she's supposed to do. When she hears the sirens or sees the flashing lights, she's supposed to pull over, right? Even if the emergency vehicle has a clear lane? Even if it's on the other side of a divided highway? Even if you're not even on the same road?

Of course not. Your responsibility is to help ensure that the vehicle in question has the right of way and a clear path to follow. But most motorists don't see it that way. They learned in driver's ed in high school, you see the flashing lights behind you, you pull over. Take great care to hear and see the siren and lights before everyone else does and adjust your position or get off the road entirely.

The Very Old and the Very Young

There is something to be said for experience. There is also something to be said for too much experience.

Remember that young drivers, especially males, are highly overrepresented in

Is this a driving enthusiast or someone trying to impress his friends? Or the girls? Either way, give these cowboys a wide berth. You can usually tell by the orientation of their baseball caps and the quantity and types of stickers on their car's windows what you're up against.

Any decal of any sort of cartoon character urinating on an automobile manufacturer's emblem should set off warning bells in your head.

crashes. (In a recent study of multivehicle fatal crashes conducted in Minnesota, a huge majority—77 percent—of the other drivers were males younger than 40.) Give these cowboys a wide berth and learn to identify them easily. You can usually tell by the orientation of their baseball caps and the quantity and types of stickers on their car's windows. Any decal of any sort of cartoon character urinating on any make of truck should set off warning bells in your head. Sports team flags and jerseys can be a dead giveaway.

Any vehicle resembling a youngster's car with four or more heads peeking up over the window line should be avoided at all costs. These people frequently drive under the influence of peer pressure. Any car driven by any old man wearing any sort of hat is a likely suspect, too. Any vehicle in which you can see that the driver's seat cover is a vest of wooden beads is one to avoid.

Unfortunately, danger also lurks inherent in older drivers. They're probably perfectly safe and competent operators, but years have a way on sneaking up on them, and things like vision, memory, hearing, and reflexes all deteriorate over time, no matter what. Expect a very old driver to be less attentive to your existence than other drivers will be, and give him or her plenty of room. Also take care to watch for those who may be frantically trying to

maneuver around a slower driver or around one who has already gaffed and is looking like they'll do it again.

Cell Phones, Cars-full, and Food

Easily identifiable, cars driven by mobile businessmen, filled with tourists, or used as internal-combustion restaurants are fairly easy to spot. Just look for the car that appears to be being steered with someone's elbows, and you know where the nearest problem driver is. It's truly comical to pass a car doing a sixpence turn on a straight stretch of asphalt—they're usually going 20 miles per hour slower than the rest of traffic and don't appear to actually be residing in this dimension—and discover that the driver is gabbing away on a cell phone, having a four-way conversation, or trying to add a packet of mayonnaise to a half-wrapped cheeseburger.

P's of S

While not true 100 percent of the time, you can usually get a good read on someone's approach to road rules and etiquette by the condition in which they maintain their car. Someone driving around with smashed fenders, missing bumpers, crap-splattered license plates, or broken windows is probably not the conscientious type you most hope to share

When you pass someone driving very slowly and weaving with little jolts left and right—they're usually going 20 miles per hour slower than the rest of the traffic and don't appear to actually be residing in this dimension—you'll notice they're almost always gabbing away on a cell phone.

Any car driven by any old man wearing any sort of hat is a likely suspect to cause problems with traffic flow. Any vehicle in which you can see that the driver's seat cover is a vest of wooden beads is one to avoid as well.

Identify your problem vehicles before they become problems.

Staring intently at something is a sure way to ignore what it's doing as a whole. Your peripheral vision is better at detecting movement than your central focus. Try it sometime. Focus on one point and see how well you detect the movement of things nearby instead.

the road with. Around here they're Escorts with pop-music bumper stickers and late-1980s Bonnevilles and Grand Ams. In Chicago, they're mid-1970s Olds Cutlasses and Delta 88s. I'm sure you've got them in your city—which models are they?

Talk Yourself Through It

When you're dealing with the worst type of hazard (a car turning into your path of travel from a standing start), every second counts. Every millisecond counts. There is yet another way to shave off even more of your reaction time in the event someone tries to add your front tire aspect to their Delta 88's dent collection. But it takes effort and practice.

You need to prepare your mind to do exactly what you should do at the exact moment you should do it. "But I already am prepared," you say. "I've slowed down, I'm in a good position, I'm covering my brakes, I'm making eye contact, I'm doing everything possible." Yes, you are. Almost. People do all these things all the time and still they T-bone Toyotas and Tahoes. I'm talking about preparing your subconscious. It's simple, but it takes a little practice.

Let's put it this way, who is going to be able to swerve faster, a motorcyclist who's thinking, "Okay, if this guy pulls out in

front of me, I'm going to swerve," or someone who's using peripheral vision to detect any movement from the vehicle, waiting for it to move forward, and thinking over and over, "Swerve. Swerve. Swerve. Swerve. Swerve." Talk yourself into a state of readiness. Like fanning the brake in an intersection to ever so slightly begin braking and compressing the forks, you are placing your mind at the point where you've made the decision already. All you have to do is let your body react. You're priming the pump, priming your synapses to welcome the swerving movement. Imagine saying to yourself over and over, "Accelerate. Accelerate. Accelerate," and when the left-turning vehicle lurches into your path, you try to use your brakes in a last-minute decision. You're less likely to execute it well. On the other hand, if you were thinking, "Stop. Stop. Stop," you'd probably have a better chance of reacting well.

But there's more to this than just swerving. Braking, as I've stated earlier, is nearly always your best choice. In a situation with another car violating your path of travel, you will always be better off going slower than faster. Slower allows you more time and space to react. Slower decreases the amount of traction you use to brake and also the amount you might use to swerve after you've

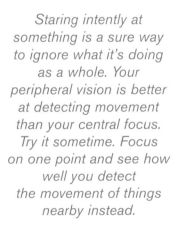

braked. Slower also reduces the severity of the injuries you'd sustain if you do collide with the vehicle. So slower is better. Always. Slower should be your first choice.

But braking is absolutely not the only choice in this situation, it's only the first choice. Once you reach the point at which you cannot stop without augering into the side of the other vehicle, you need other options. Braking, your best choice otherwise, has now become the second-best option. It's very simple. If you are too close to the vehicle when it pulls out, braking will only help you reduce impact speed and energy—you're pretty much committed to crashing into the other vehicle. There comes a point in *every* possible left-turning scenario at which the *only* way to avoid the crash is to swerve. What we're trying to find is the point at which this transition occurs.

How do you find that point? You never will, because it's different in every situation. It is possible to come close to finding it, though, and that's by talking yourself through it. Again, practice. Practice is what will make this work for you.

The Technique

As you approach the hazard, you are talking to yourself, either out loud or in your head, "Brake. Brake. Brake. Brake. Brake." When you reach the point of no return, where by swerving the other vehicle has no possibility of hitting you, you switch: "Swerve. Swerve. Swerve. Swerve. Swerve." Your mind is tuned and ready. You're primed. All it takes is the moment of movement on the hazard's part and you are *out of there*. Get it? Your body will react as fast as your mind—or at least faster than it would have if you had only a loose idea of what your plan was.

There is something more to add here, and I'll give a nod to my good friend Kent Larson for teaching me this. After you've made the mental transition between brake and swerve, there will come another tran-

sition point in which you are very, very vulnerable. If the car hasn't pulled out in front of you during the phase in which you'd either brake or swerve, the driver can still do so when it's too late for braking *or* swerving to be of any help to you.

When your plan is to swerve, there is still a way for them to get you—if they really wanted to. With perfect timing and acceleration, that turner could hit you before you'd even be able to reach your brakes, and swerving would take too long. You're a sitting duck. There seems to be nothing you can do. What do you do now?

Talk to yourself: "Go! Go! Go! Go! Go!" Use the throttle, accelerate, spend as little time in that danger area as you absolutely have to.

What you have in the case of a left-turning vehicle is a fight-or-flight decision. Your instinct wants to fight, but you must train it for flight. Rather than focusing on what the hazard may or may not be doing, view the hazard peripherally and concentrate on your flight plan.

Imagine thousands of years ago, when a caveman was confronted out in the open by a man-eating tiger. With no weapons, nowhere to run, nowhere to hide, and a gaping, snarling beast licking its jowls, will that caveman take his eyes off the tiger for even a split second? Doubtful.

Our gut response to a genuine life threat is "target fixation." It must be trained and practiced away. When faced with a fight or flight, your body *wants* to confront the threat. When facing down a 400-pound gorilla, this may be the best thing. On a motorcycle, it's exactly the wrong thing. Focus on your escape, and use your peripheral vision to track the hazard.

Before You Hit the Road

- Stereotyping can save your life.
- Remember who understands the rules and who doesn't.
- Talk yourself through it.
- Don't stare.

Bad Instinct! Bad! Imagine thousands of years ago, a caveman is confronted out in the open by a saber-toothed tiger. With no weapons nearby, nowhere to run, nowhere to hide, and a snarling, hungry beast staring him down, will that caveman take his eyes off the tiger for even a split second?

This instinctive response to a genuine life threat still exists in humans, and we hear about it all the time when we hear stories of "target fixation." When faced with a life-or-death hazard, your body wants to stare at the threat. Your mind wants to watch the enemy closely for any hints as to what it might do. When facing down a savage animal, this may be the best thing. On a motorcycle, it's exactly the wrong thing. Focus on your escape, and use your peripheral vision to track the hazard instead.

READING THE ROAD

The more predictable your riding environment is, the more likely you'll be able to negotiate it without surprises. Even unpredictable events can be made predictable. Enough time watching from a bird's eye will give you a sense of the patterns that emerge from the road. That said, I'd like to change gears for a moment and take a look at the bigger picture.

Let's look at hazard detection from a much wider angle. Pay attention sometime as you fly across the country on a sunny day. Look below you. Watch the shadow of the plane as it streaks across the landscape. It's moving fast, probably 500 knots or more. Ever notice how quickly the shadow passes through a town or city below? It doesn't stop, slow, or change direction. The shadow swoops across the buildings and roads and houses in an instant without slowing, without a thought, and keeps on going without missing a beat. A city teeming with millions of people. Swoosh! You've marked it with your shadow and are gone in less than a minute or two. A big town in the middle of the country. Whoosh! You're in it and out of it in a few moments. A tiny hamlet. A farm town. A cluster of grain elevators, a gas station, and a bunch of houses. Poof. You're there and gone in a couple seconds.

Imagine in all your travels how many houses you've passed without noticing—houses, homes, and families that never even made a dent in your consciousness. Pat Hahn

Now imagine you're on the ground, and the plane just cast its shadow across your face. Whoosh! Do those people in that plane care about you or even know you're there?

Now pay attention to it sometime when you're driving in your car or riding your motorcycle late on a sunny day. As you pass through a city, the shadow you cast flits from one building to the next, from grass to tree to house to grass to fence to house to building, darkening the surface for one brief moment before moving on just as steadily as you are. The shadow gets larger and smaller, depending on how close or far away the buildings are from you, but it never slows. You can pass through an entire city, a whole society bustling with hundreds of thousands of people, in the matter of half an hour. You can whisk through a small town with a modest population in a couple of minutes. Out on the road, in the countryside, you pass countless thousands of farmhouses, left and right, hardly ever even noticing any of them. Imagine, in all your travels, by bike or car or airplane or by whatever mode you go, imagine how many houses—residences—you've passed without noticing, houses and homes that never even made a dent in your consciousness. Or even if you observed and took note of all of them, imagine how many you've passed. Every time you go on a ride in the country, you pass hundreds—thousands even.

Now imagine you're in one of those houses, and a motorcycle glides by in the distance. Does that rider care about you, or even know you're there?

Think for a minute about your own house. How many people live there? As the hundreds and thousands of cars, motorcycles, and airplanes whiz by every day, whether they're above you or on your street or the road in the distance or the highway over the hill, do you think any of those people driving those cars give a single thought to you, your childhood, your job, your role in other people's lives, or your life? Those drivers zip by without any thought of the history taking place inside your one, single, insignificant dwelling. They drive by seeing nothing but a house, if they notice it at all. No thought of the people and the lives so far removed from their own. Planes flying overhead, darkening for one tiny instant your rooftop, then moving instantaneously on to the next house, and the next, and the next, so quickly the shadow isn't really even there—and each house is just like yours. Every house in the world has the equivalent lifetime of experiences as yours does—each family a life's work for a whole team of biographers. When we're in our cars or on our bikes, we fly past all these houses just as quickly and with as little thought as they fly past ours.

The World

The world is a big place. We think we have a pretty good idea how it is; we think we know what other people are thinking and what they're like, but do we? Do you think the woman driving by at 30 miles per hour has any idea who you are or what you think? Look inside your house. Your house has a family and a history, and it would take years to describe it to a single person. Now look outside your house. There's probably a house next door. That house has a family and a history that would also take several biographers years to write or tell another person. There's undoubtedly a house after that, and one after that, on either side, and across the street or road, and the next street over, and the next town over. Hundreds, thousands, millions of other houses just like yours—with a history and a destiny that would take a lifetime to teach fully to just one other person. (This, all without even considering whether we'd *want* to learn about them. I know I barely have the time or patience to learn about and grow with the people I do know and care about. How could I ever find time to learn even one-tenth of one percent about someone I don't even *want* to know? And what would they possibly ever want to learn about me, where I come from, who I am? They're busy with their own lives and their own histories and have absolutely no interest in what I'm up to.)

As hundreds and thousands of cars, motorcycles, and airplanes whiz by your house every day, whether they're above you or on your street or the road in the distance or the highway over the hill, do you think any of those people driving those cars give a single thought to you, your role, or your life?

Every household in the world has an equivalent lifetime of experiences as yours does—each family a life's work for a whole team of biographers. The world is a big place. We think we have a pretty good idea how it is, we think we know what other people are thinking and what they're like, but do we?

We live in this world. We know absolutely nothing about 99.9 percent of the people in it. We're surely all very, very different, and yet there is an undeniable fact: We have to share the same roadways.

Millions of people passed the same test to earn the privilege to drive—but how many passed it with any real skill or understanding? How many failed it the first try?

So we live in this world. We know absolutely nothing about 99.9 percent of the people in it. We're surely all very, very different, and yet there is an undeniable fact: We have to share the same roadways.

Everyone else who lives in this world also knows absolutely nothing about 99.9 percent of it, and is forced to share the roads with us. Millions and millions of people all trundling around in vehicles, big, heavy vehicles, metal and plastic and rubber and glass that could wipe out a whole family with one poor decision or simple instance of bad timing.

Millions of people all passed the same test to earn the privilege of driving—but how

many passed it with any real skill or understanding? How many failed it the first try? How many even think about what sharing the road means? How many understand that they're expected to stay in control of their vehicle and follow the rules? With that many people knowing so little about one another, with that many histories and reasons for existence and loves and lives and obligations, how is it possible that we can all be instantly familiar and of like minds when we're suddenly on the road together? Following the rules helps.

The Rules

I wonder when it was, exactly, that we invented our motor laws?

There probably weren't any when people walked everywhere. There probably weren't any when people rode animals—though there were probably some customs like "always pass on the left" or something like that. About that time we probably began to see our first real crashes, too—when people started riding animals, that is. Great big tremendous clattering collisions leaving bells rung and pots and pans everywhere, spilt milk and cats and dogs running amok.

Then when people started pulling wheeled carriages behind animals, it probably snowballed—the old folkways probably turned into some serious rules. If you pass on the right, people get pissed. If you crash, people get hurt. Property gets damaged. There was probably pretty strong pressure to follow the rules.

So when the first horseless carriage was built (or better yet, the horseless horse) there probably still weren't any traffic laws—only the norms and customs we'd managed to live with for hundreds and thousands of years. But when that second horseless horse was built, I bet at that very moment someone thought, "Hey, somebody's gonna get hurt. We'd better think about this." When mass production got going, I'll bet that's when it really all started. Stay on that side of the road and yield to the person on the right at the crossroads. They probably said, "There. That oughta take care of it."

Where you are a motorcycle enthusiast, others are family enthusiasts or work enthusiasts. The roads are jammed with people who only think hard about driving when they have to, and usually not while driving.

Roads aren't designed for fun; they are designed to get you somewhere safely with as little trouble as possible. Predictable is good. Surprises are bad.

But that didn't take care of it, and it didn't stop there. In a world this big, filled with millions and millions of travelers, leaving it at that would have been far too simple.

With zillions of unique beings clogging the roads, there had to be some rules. We developed a complex system of do-thisses and don't-do-thats to help people navigate and to keep things predictable. After all, the roads weren't designed for fun; they were designed to get you somewhere safely and with as little trouble as possible. Predictable is good. Surprises are bad.

You, reading this book: You're a motorcyclist—you're an enthusiast. You have a great appreciation for the road and the route and the area between point A and point B. You, as someone who derives great pleasure from skillfully negotiating the road and the curves and the hills, probably expect the other people using the road to do the same.

But think about the other millions of people and their other million backgrounds and ideas about what's important. Most of them don't care a whit about the road. It's solely Point A and Point B. Where you are a motorcycle or motorsports enthusiast, these others are family enthusiasts or work enthusiasts. The roads are filled with people who only think about the road or about driving when they

absolutely have to (usually, *not* while they're driving), like in traffic school. They think about it only when they're forced to.

When asked how they rate themselves versus other drivers, most people will reply that they are "above average." And they believe it, too. But other than that moment when they're asked, they're off in la-la land, doing their non-motorcycle-enthusiast thing, because that's what's important to them. The road is meaningless in their world. This life-giving, entertaining, funnest-distance-between-two-points slab of asphalt we all travel is only a means to an end to these people. They could be UFO enthusiasts. Or church enthusiasts. They could be shootout enthusiasts. Who knows how many lawn enthusiasts there are who are probably wondering, "Why doesn't that guy mow his lawn more #!&*ing often?" Many of these people don't even realize there is even such a thing as a good road or understand the significance of the rules, etiquette, signs, or risks—or consequences, should they go and do something wrong. A good road is one that goes exactly where they want it to go. Rules are for other people, something to help them play golf. Or more likely something about which they are totally ignorant.

Get the idea? You're in the minority. You're more unusual. Your history and

This entertaining, funnest-distance-between-two-points slab of asphalt we travel is only a means to an end to some people. They could be UFO enthusiasts, or church enthusiasts, or living-in-the-past enthusiasts.

Motorcycle heaven. No speed limits. The roads are all smooth, sticky, and banked positively in the corners. Pat Hahn

The point of the rules is that everybody knows *those rules and everybody does the same thing, every time, all the time.*

your family and your household are unique. No one knows you. You know nothing about everybody else. But they're also unique, as you are. Your only possible common bond when you're on the road is the set of rules you follow. It's important to remember this when you're out there. Assuming everyone else sees it the way you do is a bad idea.

Let's say you're going to start your own country. At the equator, where it's motorcycle season year-round. And it's motorcycles only. No cars, trucks, tractors, or sandy salt trucks. Motorcycle heaven. Everybody rides to work. Everybody carves 'em on weekends. No speed limits. The roads are all smooth, sticky, and banked positively in the corners. Shoulders are all paved. Gas is cheap. Insurance is free.

Sounds great, doesn't it? The trouble is, everybody's doing their own thing and sharing the road while they're doing it.

So you've got to have some rules to keep things predictable. So nobody brings an early end to what promises to be an endless riding season, and so you don't end anybody else's riding season. You've got to make it predictable. You've got to get everybody going in the same direction.

First things first—on which side of the road should everybody ride? Let's arbitrarily choose the right side. This in itself solves most of the problems. Its impact on public safety is obvious. Nobody in their right mind would argue with it. Because of this rule, everybody knows what

to do when meeting an oncoming bike, and everybody knows what to do when overtaking. The point is, everybody *knows*, and everybody does the same thing, every time, all the time. Life is good, and life is *very* predictable.

This works out so well that you make other rules. Intersections get stop signs, ramps get yield signs, and everything's decked out in colored lights. This all makes pretty good sense. Alcohol becomes a no-no for those riding. You make up rules for passing, and rules for following. There are rules for how old you have to be. (In modern societies, they even make rules to protect you from yourself. We won't have any of that here. You can do whatever you like to *yourself,* so long as you don't take anybody else with you. Leave it to the modern, civilized societies to try to usurp natural selection. There'll be *none* of that.) It's all laid out, it's all predictable, it's all good.

The River

The problem is that we can't have Planet Motorcycle. We're stuck with Planet Everybody, a.k.a Planet Earth. Is there a way to make it as predictable as Planet Motorcycle? No way. But there is a way to see the patterns a little more clearly.

Imagine a river flowing from the mountains to the ocean. The relentless flow of water follows the simplest course it can find, always seeking its destination, detouring around things it can't go over or through. The water carries with it boulders, pebbles, sand, and silt, moving it along at about the same speed as the water—or at least moving at the pace that the water and land dictate.

A road is essentially a river of traffic. The flow is continual, sometimes clogged with its load, sometimes clear, but always moving. The speed at which traffic moves is dictated by the road and the land through which it travels.

But what happens when you place an obstruction in the water? Take for example a simple, gradual bend in the river. When the water reaches the bend and the direction changes, the debris—the boulders, pebbles, sand, silt—wants to continue flowing forward. It begins to bunch up, tumble over itself, collide, grind against itself, and it fights to get through, to continue to force everything through with the pace that the river sets. Some of the load needs to go faster to keep the pace, some slower. A bend in the river changes the dynamic and forces the same load to flow through essentially less space and with less freedom to adjust to the bend. Around a river bend, you see friction and collisions between particles in the river that would otherwise flow freely. You see debris pile up on the slow side (the inside) and get washed violently away on the fast side (the outside).

Placing an obstruction of any kind onto a road will change the flow of traffic—whether a merge area, bend, or slow-moving vehicle. A curve, for example, forces the inside load of traffic to travel slower and the outside load to travel faster in order to maintain the same overall pace. The traffic's natural tendency is to continue straight ahead, and drivers need to fight the forces of physics in order to remain on the road.

In a river, bends are natural and happen all the time. They're inevitable. Sometimes the land creates them, sometimes the river itself creates them. The water always turns them into something new. The river meanders—the thousand-year evolution of a straight river into an endless series of oxbow switchbacks—is one of the true marvels of geological phenomena. A road designed the same way is one of the true thrills of modern engineering.

So what about a "true" break in the flow? What about a foreign obstruction forced suddenly into the flow? Try dropping a nonmoving boulder into the river. It works just like a bend, in that the debris needs to flow by, but it is resistant to changing direction. The boulder also snatches away some of the space the debris has to flow. But where a bend can allow the particles to adjust their speed and space and still continue along with the flow, dropping some off on the inside and picking some more up on the outside, now the sand and

silt and pebbles and other boulders smash into the boulder you just dropped in the river. Now the surge of water and all its accompanying debris work relentlessly to try to move it along, creating eddies and swirling and collisions and violence in the process.

So what happens when you drop a slow or nonmoving vehicle into a steady flow of traffic? The same thing that happens in a river. The rest of the load has to fight to get around it, and it usually works some violence on the obstacle in question.

The turbulence brought on by this one obstacle changes a great deal about the overall flow. It's a glitch in the big system. It's a monkey wrench in the river's, and the road's, plan. The river and the debris, however, are the norm, they are the majority, and they work and grind the boulder away, a little at a time, into nothing. The road and the traffic are the same way, by design, grinding away at the slow-moving vehicle and each other to continue on toward point B. The intrusion of the obstacle creates carnage and destruction for itself and that which strikes it. It also creates violence and turmoil for everything else disturbed by the new wakes and eddies, the new foreign turbulence that has been added to the overall harmonious flow.

Get the idea? The water wants to flow, wants to keep going, and intrusive objects, big or small, that don't go along with the flow cause a lot of trouble with the movement of the river and the load that it carries. Breaks in the flow inevitably leave destruction in their wake.

Breaks in the Flow

So imagine the river is the road. What can cause a break in the flow?

A straight road, in theory, should flow smoothly and evenly. Add a curve and what happens? A break in the flow. Minor, navigable, but not the same as the straight and narrow, so things aren't quite so harmonious. In the curves, things start to bunch up.

An intersection also creates a break in the flow. Crossing traffic and control signals act like big boulders dropped onto the road. Another example is a merge ramp. Slower vehicles try to share space

A bend in the river changes the dynamics and forces the same load to flow through essentially less space and with less freedom to adjust to the bend.

The traffic wants to flow, wants to keep going, and intrusive objects, big or small, that don't go along with the flow cause a lot of trouble.

Crossing traffic and control signals act like big boulders dropped onto the road.

Imagine what a "safe" road would look like—one designed to have no crashes at all. The road would be perfectly straight, with no intersections of any sort.

already occupied by too many vehicles. Speed zones. Emergency vehicles. Cops sitting at the roadside or sitting in the left lane at 55. Bicyclists, animals, pedestrians, other vehicles, slow vehicles, fast vehicles, surface hazards, construction areas. These all cause breaks in the flow of the road and the traffic.

Imagine what a safe road would look like—one designed to have no crashes at all. (It's never going to happen, but let's imagine anyway.) The road would be perfectly straight, with no intersections of any sort. One slab of asphalt, in a line, stretching as far as the eye can see. (Well, until you hit the mountains.) The whole thing would be fenced off to prevent animals and pedestrians from interfering with the flow of traffic. Everyone would travel at the same speed, whatever that might be. Assuming that, and assuming no one would need to ever get on or off the road, with all these things, would there still be crashes? Is it possible to crash-proof a road?

Of course there'd be crashes. There's no way to crash-proof a road. Even with everything controlled just so, with no reasons of any sort for anyone to do anything different than drive in a straight line and do it safely, there'd still be crashes. That's life—to be imperfect and unpredictable and turn upside-down at precisely the wrong moment. Remember, we're millions of different types of enthusiasts all using the same roads. Even on this mythological highway where everyone goes the same speed and everything's straight and narrow and there are no surprises, people would still fall asleep at the wheel or have a blowout or have a cardiac arrest and swerve into the oncoming lane.

A crash-proof road could never happen.

Build a controlled-access highway as straight and as smooth as you want, enact as many laws and drop in as few breaks in the flow as you want, give everyone good etiquette and good education, and there will still be crashes. People make mistakes. And if a straight road can never be crash-proof, what can we say about the curvy country roads that are so much fun for motorcyclists?

Deviations

I'm talking about deviations. Deviations are what cause crashes. Breaks in the flow are deviations. Obstructions are deviations. Deviations happen when the straight and narrow and predictable has to bend, as it inevitably will, to reality. A perfectly straight road, fenced off completely, where everyone travels at the same speed and behaves the same way is more likely to be found in a fairy tale than in even the most outrageous idealism. There is no "normal" without "deviation."

Curves are deviations. Intersections are deviations. Merge ramps, speed zones, emergency vehicles, cops, bicyclists, animals, pedestrians, faster vehicles, slower vehicles, potholes, construction zones—they're all deviations. The roads can't be straight all the time, and they can't be all about motorcyclists all the time. You're an enthusiast on a road full of users. You are a diehard in a world full of doers. You are forced to make a compromise and use the same roads as the other zillion people that also need to use them. You need to share the road with millions and millions of deviants.

Two Deviations from Hell

Where do you see the two worst everyday deviations?

• Emergency vehicles (fire trucks and ambulances, primarily)

• Ramps (usually the point beneath the overpass)

If you're trying to lower your risks by avoiding situations in which people are likely to deviate and cause serious breaks in the flow, these two should be at the top of your list. Generally, they're because people just don't get the point of the whole thing.

When most drivers see the flashing lights of a fire engine or emergency vehicle, what do they do? They completely lose their minds. Without thinking or looking over their shoulder, they slam on the brakes with both feet and veer as far off the road as they possibly can without actually running into the ditch or hitting a light pole. I'm sure they're trying to do the right thing, but they no longer understand what the right thing is—to clear a path for the emergency vehicle. Instead, they remember their driver's ed teacher yelling at them, "If there's flashing lights, pull over!" Don't expect that just because the oncoming ambulance has two full, clear lanes to use doesn't mean that the car whose blind spot you're riding in won't swerve to clear an even bigger path.

One of the funniest (not funny-ha-ha, but funny-sad) scenes I ever saw was while waiting at a light in heavy traffic at a four-lane, four-way intersection controlled by stoplights. A strobe light from an approaching ambulance triggered all the lights to go red. So there we were, rush-hour traffic, every lane clogged 10 cars deep and waiting at a red light, and a frantically shrieking emergency vehicle trying to get through. Every driver wanted desperately to move aside but was blocked by another car or the curb or the median. No one would move forward, terrified of violating the red light (even though it was clear that it was red in every direction). It was a complete stalemate. Everyone near me sat, looking anxiously into their rearview mirrors, while the hapless ambulance driver could do nothing but honk and wait. When can a red light mean go!

Another place you'll see misinformed motorists creating breaks in the flow and horrible speed deviations is in merging areas—especially on freeways. There is always someone who drives down the ramp, looking as if they're going to smoothly merge with traffic, but then instead use both feet to stomp the brake and bring the vehicle to a complete halt, right where the ramp and the freeway meet. They're supposed to yield the right of way, so they'll park and wait for an opening. Very polite, I must say. They simply don't understand that the purpose of the merge ramp is to gather speed to blend smoothly with the flow.

Even with no reasons of any sort for anyone to do anything different than drive in a straight line and do it safely, there'd still be crashes.

If a straight road can never be crash-proof, what can we say about the curvy country roads that are so much fun on a motorcycle or the clogged roads upon which we must commute?

125

Unfortunately, highway designers have decided that since no one knows how to merge anyway, they must force us to at least spread out a little bit.

When scanning for hazards, look for the person doing something different than everyone else is doing. If there's going to be a crash, it's likely to be in that vicinity. If they're doing something dramatically different, there's liable to be some serious consequences for those involved.

This creates multiple problems, including potential rear-end collisions among the vehicles behind them on the ramp, and inevitable sudden slowdown and lane changing by those on the freeway when they suddenly dart into the flow at 50 miles per hour less than the rest of the traffic. They also bring with them a half-dozen other vehicles, all traveling at the same speed (50 shy of the norm), all pissed off, and all following within half a car length of one another while trying to look over their shoulders. Now combine this cluster-flock of deviants with the poor saps trying to exit at the same time—a sudden need to slow by about 50 miles per hour, no room to move into the exit lane, and no room with which to do it. That, and you've got everyone who's not exiting trying to move left to avoid having to slow down. This is a crash just waiting to happen. This happens all the time, too, at ramps where meters are placed too close to the merging area.

The second-funniest thing I've ever seen is a lonely economy car waiting on a wide-open, multilane, on ramp at a meter. It was early afternoon, the beginning of rush hour, and there was little traffic. With the line of sight I had, I could see this car from far away, just sitting there at the ramp meter. No other cars were in sight, and

there was no traffic to speak of—it was just sitting there. The right-hand meter flipped to green and then back to red, and the car lurched and then slammed on the brakes. The driver was unfortunately waiting for the left-hand meter, and that one wasn't the one that changed, so the driver continued to wait. I rarely laugh out loud when I'm riding, but I did that day. By the time I was about a half-mile farther, I checked my mirror again and the driver was still there waiting. There's such a huge difference sometimes between the letter and the spirit of the rules.

Back Into The River

As the river creates violence on that which impedes its flow, so does the flow of traffic on a deviation on its roadway. A driver breaking away from the norm on the road is the same as a boulder dropped into a river. It creates a break in the flow and sets the stage for much turbulence, violence, and force—a temporary situation just begging to be rectified. Imagine a straight road, with everybody going about 60 miles per hour. The knucklehead going 30 miles per hour is the deviant and is about to cause a great deal of trouble for the rest of the flow. People may not crash into the deviant (unless he or she begins adding additional

Just the fact that they have to post the minimum speed on a sign gives me the willies.

deviant behaviors to his or her driving), but they'll surely crash into each other trying to force their way around the deviant. Maybe not the first car, maybe not the second, but on the endless straight highway, someone, somewhere, will also be deviating at the same time (that's two risk factors coming together) and *bam*! Now you've got violence. Multivehicle crashes happen when one or more drivers deviate from the norm and cause a break in the flow.

As motorists, we are fairly used to normal deviations. The speeds, tolerances, advisories, two-second following distance, etc., at which we use the roads allow us to manage and accommodate most standard deviations, even though they still create obvious and disharmonious breaks in the flow. Standard deviations are the norm out on the road and are to be expected. Remember, everyone else is unique, just as you are. Everyone's an enthusiast of some sort, and not necessarily of the driving type. Everyone has his or her own place, time, destination, pace, habits, abilities, destiny, and history. One deviation is typical and usually manageable.

A risk factor—a break in the flow, a deviation, or some other risk factor—is usually not a problem. It's when they're combined that outcomes get less predictable and more dangerous. Imagine someone traveling 30 miles per hour in a 50-miles-per-hour zone. One deviation, no big deal. Everyone goes around them. Now add another deviation: someone not realizing

that the first person's only going 30 until they're almost on top of them. Surprise! They swerve quickly to avoid hitting them but without checking their blind spot first—two deviations. Still not the end of the world. But let's add another: if the person next to the swerver isn't paying close-enough attention (three deviations), they may find themselves in a bad position—*smash*! The second car swerves into the third—*screech!*—the third car brakes hard to avoid the collision. The chain reaction can end there or it can continue—if a fourth person behind the third one wasn't paying attention either, *smash*! Rear-end accident. And so on. Add a sharp curve and steep drop-off to the mix and how much worse does it get? Add alcohol to the mix and how much worse does it get?

Two deviations are where the real problems begin. Whether someone deviates twice as much from the norm, or deviates two different ways at the same time, or if two people deviate at the same time and the same place—that's where the multivehicle crashes happen. Deviations are also risk factors. One risk factor is usually not a problem. Two are the beginning of a problem. More than two and you have some serious risk. Throw in a couple standard deviations with a few simultaneous risk factors, and you've got a problem that's about to be resolved in the worst way. Deviations pile up and cause trouble.

The roadway is like a river where everything is more or less forced to go along with the flow. Every roadway, like every river, has structural obstacles that cause breaks in the flow and contribute to crashes. Humans by nature are unique. Living in their own worlds, they cause further breaks in the flow by their own standard deviations. Adding risk factors makes these breaks in the flow and standard deviations more dangerous. Know your risk factors.

A risk factor—a break in the flow, a deviation, or some other risk factor—is usually not a problem. It's when risk factors are combined that outcomes get less predictable and more dangerous.

Law enforcement's primary purpose is to preserve harmony by singling out deviant behavior and putting a stop to it. Of course, law enforcement officers may have different ideas about what's deviant and what's not. . . .

The road is like a river, in that everyone is more or less forced to go along with the flow. Every roadway, like every river, has structural obstacles that cause breaks in the flow and contribute to crashes. Humans are unique and cause further breaks in the flow by their own standard deviations. That's nature. Pat Hahn

Keep an eye on the larger pattern.

Learn to recognize where the breaks in the flow are. Learn to recognize the deviants. See the problems before they affect you, and take steps to avoid the whole situation. It doesn't matter who does what, only that you are aware they're going to cause problems for everyone else. Learn to look past the behavior and the circumstances and focus on your own safety. You won't change their behavior anyway. Know where you are in relation to the problem and place yourself out of harm's way.

And do your best to not be a deviant.

Rider Prescience

New rule: When something makes you frown, you'd better slow it down.

I sometimes momentarily fixate on things that are unusual. I suspect everybody does. You see something that doesn't quite jibe with your memory or your sense of how things should be. You sense something that isn't usually there or something that

shouldn't be there. You make a little frown, your brows knit for a minute, the gears turn in your head.

Your subconscious is telling you something's wrong. You don't realize what it is, something just sort of catches your attention and you kind of stare at it, giving it a closer look. You concentrate, trying to recognize what you see.

All the while you're heading toward it at 88 feet per second. (It's kind of like when someone changes the subject midsentence, and it takes your brain about three seconds to establish the new context and understand the words. They might as well be in a foreign language.) When it's too late to realize why it doesn't look right, something happens to wreck your day.

One morning, complacently rolling along a low-traffic road in the left lane at about 60, I watched a dump truck pull out of an old gas station, turning right, toward me, on the opposite side of the divided four-lane. There was no big deal. But something caught my eye. The turn, something

New rule: When something makes you frown, you'd better slow it down.

128

about the turn, just wasn't quite right. The angle was somehow wrong. I then realized, "Oh. It's turning left. I get it."

But something wasn't quite right. I still hadn't got it. At this particular interchange, there are islands in place for motorists turning left or right out of there, presumably to guide them away from oncoming traffic.

The dump truck had somehow started into the right turn, but then the driver decided that she needed to turn left. That's what I was looking at, but I couldn't quite figure it out because it was so unusual. This woman, who obviously had learned to drive on Venus or Jupiter or some planet where head-on-collisions are not usually a problem, was turning directly into oncoming traffic.

All the while, I'm staring, fascinated, trying to understand what's going on, and moving at 88 feet per second. Warning! Warning! Danger! Danger! Deviant on the loose!

So this dimwit turned right and pointed herself right into my headlight, then realized her mistake, and cranked the dump truck hard left, around the island, and into the far right lane, finally and thankfully going my direction—at about 20 miles per hour. "Oh, now I get it. She was going to turn right and then changed her mind." I relaxed on the throttle and slowed slightly to allow her room to fully clear my lane and get pointed in the right direction.

But I had forgotten she was a deviant. Stupid moves often come in pairs! Mary the truck driver from Pluto then veered suddenly *back* into my lane for some dumb reason. Still not quite sure what I had been seeing and momentarily bewildered, I had to shake myself out of it and make a very quick and thorough speed reduction to avoid bashing into the left-rear mudflap of the truck. I'd also concentrated so hard on just what the heck was going on up there I lost track of who was behind me. It turns out no one, but I consider it lucky I didn't become a motorcycle sandwich.

The whole event really wasn't even a close call, but it was a good reminder.

When someone does something stupid, it's likely that person's not too bright and will probably do something equally stupid in the very near future, and probably when you're close enough to get hurt. This sleepy idiot with my life in her hands made a stupid turn, then corrected, and then immediately made a stupid and unnecessary lane change. It was unusual, puzzling, but most of all, *frown inducing*.

Moral of the story: When something makes you frown, you'd better slow it down.

When you see something that puzzles you, you need to instinctively reduce your speed until you know for sure what's going on. Be aware of those times when your brain is spending too much time trying to solve a puzzle on the road. Ever noticed someone driving really, really slow and sort of hugging on the right edge of the right lane? In the time that it takes you to think, "What in the world is this idiot doing?" he or she has already begun their illegal U-turn.

Do this even if you consciously think you don't need to. If it makes you frown, you're operating at less than full observational potential. Something like 40 percent of the fatalities in the Hurt Study were riders who made no defensive move at all. That's complacency.

Do it automatically. Program yourself. You have to recognize that your mind is distracted, working on something that probably isn't about riding, and you need to adapt to it so as not to put yourself into a bad situation.

I remember reading years ago about some kid who died when a big dump truck U-turned on the freeway in front of him. I can just imagine him thinking, moments before his life ended, "Why is that big truck stopped along the inside shoulder over there?" as he raced toward it at 88 feet per second.

Before You Hit the Road
- Remember, most road users aren't road enthusiasts like you.
- Watch for breaks in the flow.
- Keep an eye out for deviants.
- When something makes you frown, you'd better slow it down.

When you see something that puzzles you, you need to instinctively reduce your speed until you know for sure what's going on.

chapter 13

GROUP RIDING AND OTHER DISTRACTIONS

Throughout this book, we've worked hard to make our way down the Risk Level Table from 10 to the lowest possible of Risk Level 2. For this next-to-last chapter, I want to look at it another way.

Every rider is always somewhere between zero and 100 percent safety, or riding efficiency, at any given time. Actually, perfect efficiency and perfect inefficiency are not achievable, so we'll say every rider is somewhere between 1 and 99 percent, instead.

One percent would probably look like some suicidal numbnuts riding at Risk Level 10—drunk, without gear, skills, or a strategy, weaving in and out of rush-hour traffic on the freeway—with every car driver deliberately trying to kill that rider. Ninety-nine, on the other hand, would appear more as a conscientious, skilled motorcyclist using all three degrees of separation, the knowledge gained from numerous riding schools, motorcycle books, articles, and this book, riding sedately in an area of sparse population in the southwestern United States.

Everything else is somewhere in between. Every time you ride, you're somewhere between zero and 100. But how do you tell where exactly you are?

Every time you ride, you're somewhere between zero and 100 percent safety or riding efficiency. But how do you tell where exactly you are?

Sometimes your plan fails and you have to ride during a high-risk time. Where you would normally be riding at, say, 75 percent efficiency, the new traffic patterns and behavior and later hour put you at a lower level, more like 60.

One percent could also look like a rider going 100 miles per hour in a 10-miles-per-hour zone filled with pedestrians carrying big, long two-by-fours and spilling sand all over the asphalt. Ninety-nine percent could look like the same rider going zero in the same 10-miles-per-hour zone. To see the way risk increases simply with speed, imagine how much additional risk the rider faces when he or she begins moving away from zero miles per hour. Two miles per hour. Five miles per hour. Ten miles per hour. And so on. Every single factor you add into your riding takes you up the scale. Every additional mile per hour decreases your safety.

Sadly, you you'll never be able to know where you are on the scale. You can only estimate, and even that is a leap of faith not meant to measure, only to illustrate. But what it can do is help you see clearly the things that move you up and down the scale and help you

take steps to eliminate them. Let's say, for argument's sake, that the average rider's base percentage of safety is 50 percent on any given day. How do minor risks change it?

Let's start with visibility. You've followed the advice in Chapter 6 and work hard to keep your main source of information free from harm. But suddenly, you enter a tunnel after a half-hour of riding in the glaring sunshine and you, and everyone around you, are momentarily blinded. That, for example, might move you down to 40 percent for a brief period of time. As everyone's eyes adjust, you slowly climb back up the scale: 41, 42, 43. . . . By the time you're back up at 50, you all emerge from the tunnel, are momentarily blinded, and have to start over again at 40.

How about your route? You're using the safest route you can think of with all the easiest turns and most predictable traffic patterns, and you're suddenly

Every way in which you remove yourself from total concentration, you move yourself down the scale, away from 99 percent riding efficiency.

Group riding is a mixed bag. On one hand, you have added visibility and backup in case of trouble. On the other hand, you have a mix of experience levels and the threat of ego and testosterone (not usually a problem on all-women group rides).

Some risks, such as group riding, poor-weather riding, and sightseeing, stem from our own natural inability to completely concentrate 100 percent of the time. Every way in which you remove yourself from total concentration, you move yourself down the scale, away from 99 percent riding efficiency.

When riding in a group, you face increased risk primarily in the form of distraction, so you make up for it with decreasing your risks elsewhere, such as speed or space cushioning. You also warn others of the risk and ask that they do the same.

stuck with a detour that takes you through a construction zone. The other drivers are even more confused than you, and you're unfamiliar with the new road. You just jumped from 50 to 45 percent safety.

Time of day? Instead of leaving work at your normal time, just prior to rush hour, you're stuck working late and forced to mix it up with 5 p.m. traffic. There again, you went from 50 to, say, 42.5 percent safety. What if you have to work so late you're riding after dark, say, at 1 a.m.? You went from 50 to 25 percent. What if you only got half as much sleep the night before and you're out past your bedtime?

The possibilities are endless. Consider also the same effect that the inability to read a road, the inability to stereotype, a new type of trouble area you'd never considered, or any number of distractions could have on your level of safety. Most times these distractions won't ever make a difference in reality. But they always make a difference in theory. If your goal is to reduce risk, you have to play the game and use the theory to your advantage.

Assuming you're using the three degrees

of separation and understand the other rider-related risks outlined in this book, it's critical to remember that not all of the remaining risks are caused by the other guy. Most are, but some, such as group riding, poor-weather riding, and sightseeing, stem from our own natural inability to completely concentrate 100 percent of the time. Every way in which you remove yourself from total concentration, you move yourself down the scale, away from 99 percent riding efficiency. Fortunately, there is still much you can do to take your risk down to the lowest possible level by using self-analysis and keeping track of your mind and body.

Group Riding

As a rule, anything that moves you away from 100 percent attention should be avoided. Group riding has the potential of distracting you (and every other rider in the group), taking you up the risk level scale or away from 99 percent efficiency. Therefore, group riding should be avoided.

But it's not as easy as that. Group riding can be a terrific amount of fun and a great

Sure, he may look normal, but pay attention to the nonverbal cues he sends you in order to assess his riding style and how much risk he'll pose to you and the group.

way to meet new people and see new sights. Like all else motorcycle, the risk-averse rider is faced with yet another compromise. You face increased risk in the form of distraction, so you make up for it with decreasing your risks elsewhere, such as speed or space cushioning, for example.

What you have to deal with when you ride in a group is a mixed bag. Whooping it up in the rolling countryside with other enthusiasts can enhance and detract from your safety at the same time. You decrease your risk by having others there to help you if you run into trouble. They also add to your visibility and prominence on the road. There is real merit to the concept of safety in numbers. An errant driver might pull a deliberate bad move on a lone motorcyclist, but would he or she necessarily try it with a large group of witnesses? Probably not. It's easy to single a loner out for malicious mistreatment, but it's entirely another thing to be the deviant drawing attention to yourself.

On the other hand, a dozen other bikes and riding styles, the added mental task of leading or tailgunning a ride, or the

thought that there's a green rider or one new to group riding directly behind you can be a tremendous distraction. Add to that the mix of experience levels, the cumbersome nature of a group, the dual threats of peer pressure and testosterone, other-rider target fixation, and the uncanny ability of otherwise sane and risk-averse riders to get in over their heads, and you've just added a whole lot of risk to your ride in exchange for a marginal amount of added safety and enjoyment. (The extra enjoyment can also be a distraction, albeit possibly a beneficial one.) On top of everything else, there's the fun of socializing during pit stops, sniffing bikes, swapping motorcycles, watching and following other riders, and learning new routes and roads.

So from the very narrow safety perspective, group riding simply isn't a very good idea. It carries with it too much additional risk for too little additional enjoyment. The tradeoff simply isn't even. You just never know when the distractions are going to all add up and cost you a crash. However, it is possible, with a little knowledge and better

Group Riding Rule Number 1: Ride your own ride. Everyone chooses his or her own pace. Everyone chooses his or her own lines. Everyone is responsible for his or her own safety.

133

The simplest way to keep the group together is to have each rider wait for the next rider at every turn.

Group Riding Rule Number 2: Pick your friends. Ride with people you know and trust. If someone gives you the willies, it's probably for a good reason. Give the potential offender plenty of room or leave the group.

Group Riding Rule Number 3: Agree beforehand on the pace, route, and procedures.

awareness of the problems, to minimize the risks posed by riding en masse.

Ride Your Own Ride
The real hinge in whether a group ride is safe or not is the degree to which each participant can ride his or her own ride. Even though a rider is part of a larger gathering, he or she is still riding on a public road and is still responsible for his or her own safety. Just being in a parade of sorts doesn't make the road any softer or more forgiving, other drivers any more skilled or less likely to pull bonehead maneuvers, or critters like a deer or dog any less likely to choose your bike as its next life lesson. When riding in numbers, ride the bike, ride the road, and ride the way you would if you were completely alone.

Recommended reading for riding your own ride is *The Pace* by Nick Ienatsch.

Pick Your Friends
Some of us are lucky enough to choose who we ride with. Others are not so lucky and have to take what they can get. Pay attention to weird vibes, subtle nonverbals, and instinct. Remember the aphorism, "When something makes you frown, better slow it down." Or in the case of a group ride, just get away from the frown-inducing person altogether, even if it means leaving the group.

If you ride only with people you know and trust, the group has more buy-in to the situation. There is more of an aura of mutual respect, responsibility, and peer pressure to make the group ride successful. Riders in a group of friends will likely be more conscious of one another than in a group of strangers, and that goes a long way to improving your safety on a group ride.

Agree Beforehand

There's nothing more chaotic or pathetically slow to move than a group that's unprepared. The last thing a motorcyclist who has one day off a week needs is to be waiting for someone who doesn't know what's going on or just exactly what the heck is expected of them. A rider like this, or a group full of them, is a huge distraction.

Agree to the pace of the ride and break large groups into smaller ones based on comfort level. Groups should consist of absolutely no more than four or five riders. Anything bigger than that poses a safety hazard, because other motorists will trip over themselves to get into the middle of the group.

Discuss the route and provide maps or route sheets. Find out who in the group doesn't know how to read one and assign them a guide who does. If the group isn't using a map or a route sheet, discuss the procedure for staying together. For example, the leader waits at each major route change for the very last rider to appear and give a thumbs-up before proceeding, or each rider waits at each turnoff for the person behind them before *proceeding*.

Whatever you decide, make sure each member of the group is certain that they won't get left behind. This is Key Number One in keeping slower riders from riding over their heads. The comfort in knowing they can ride their own slow pace and still remain with the group works miracles on new riders' confidence and ability to learn and keep up. It's also one less distraction for them. They're already at a relative disadvantage because they're new—worrying about getting lost or abandoned will only make things worse and pull them down the efficiency scale.

It's a good idea to lay out beforehand the procedure for dealing with breakdowns, gas or food stops, emergency stops, and law-enforcement stops. Doing so will economize these events and make for less decision making when the time comes. Simpler is better. Breakdowns happen from time to time, but you don't need 10 bikes surrounding the sputtering, smoking pile of junk in order to fix it. Spread out, park where you can, and walk over to try and help.

For any kind of stop, choose a place with ample room for the whole group, away from traffic and blind turns, in case anyone is following you closely to see where you park. The best advice for unplanned enforcement stops is to meet up at the next turnoff or planned stop. Staying together might risk additional performance awards, so make sure everyone knows that even though the group is gone, they'll be waiting around the corner.

Slow Down in the Straights

Faster, more experienced riders will naturally begin to put some distance between themselves and the slower riders when the road gets twisty. To help keep the group together, the faster riders should slow down in the straightaways between curvy sections. This will help allow you to concentrate fully on the relatively risky curves because the slower speed will give you more time and space to prepare for the turns, rather than maintaining a blinding speed throughout and having the curves come at you rapid fire.

The real joy of riding is curves, anyway. If you prefer to go fast in the straights and slow in the corners, maybe motorcycling isn't the best choice for you. Maybe drag racing is.

Slowing down in the straights is Key Number Two for keeping slower riders from riding over their heads. Seeing the group disappearing farther and farther into the distance on a challenging, winding road can create anxiety and produce a red mist that will keep the rider from concentrating fully and staying within his or her limits. However, if you reduce your speed on the straights (straight roads being boring at any speed, anyway) to allow the slower riders to catch up between twisty sections, this will be yet another way to remove a distraction from their minds and allow them to better concentrate on riding the bike.

Spread Out and Pass Safely

Just because you're riding with other motorcyclists doesn't mean you have to sacrifice your personal space. Nor does it mean that you can make hairball passes to get ahead of a slower rider. Spread out.

Group Riding Rule Number 4: Slow in the straights. They're boring anyway.

Group Riding Rule Number 5: Spread out and pass safely. You still need room to react to surprises.

135

If you prefer to go fast in the straights and slow in the corners, maybe motorcycling isn't the best choice for you. Maybe drag racing is.

Give other riders the room they need to speed up, slow down, find their lines, and avoid hazards. Never follow another rider any closer than they are following someone else. And don't go in for that riding side-by-side nonsense. Too many surprised riders crash into too many even-more-surprised riders every year. Riding next to your buddy might look cool, but doing so erases about one-third of your potential escape routes and goes against the basic premise of this book.

Use the "slow in the straights" rule to put some real estate between you and the rider ahead of you, widening a gap that may have narrowed during that last twistybit. After a series of curves, take a quick glance into your mirror to see if you may be holding someone up. It's both safe and polite to wave them by. Move over to the right side of your lane and let them get past you. This way you won't be tempted to look into your mirrors during a technical series of curves, the rider behind you won't be tempted to follow you too closely, and you'll both be able to enjoy riding at your own pace. Never, ever pass a new rider in a curve. Two words: instant overload.

check your mirrors only on the straight sections and then only every 5 to 10 seconds at most. The mirror lesson is also Key Number Three for slower riders. Implore them to forget about their mirrors in the twisties and check them only after the road has straightened and they have slowed down. Then they'll have the extra concentration they'll need to wave other riders past. When negotiating tricky curves, they need all the concentration they can get.

Use One Signal

When you're riding your own ride, a variety of hand signals is usually not necessary. I don't know why, but I laugh every time I see a parade of riders all pointing at a dead animal. When you're riding your own ride, you have enough space between you and the rider in front of you to see the animal without any help from anyone else. You don't point out dead animals when riding alone, so why should you on a group ride?

Sometimes, it is a nice gesture to warn riders behind you of a hazard on the road. The safest signal I can imagine is a brake light. It takes very little effort, you don't need to remove either hand from the bars, and it's unmistakable to those behind you. Red light equals something not ordinary equals slow down. Agree to it beforehand. If you're in the habit of riding smoothly—slowly in the straights, liquid in your transitions, engine braking to set up for corners, gentle inputs to maintain a large traction reserve and reduce the wear and tear on your bike—you'll find you very rarely need to use your brakes at all. And riders behind you will get used to that.

On a group ride, if you're a smooth rider, any flash of a brake light means "Something might be up: pay attention." That's a lot to say with just a light squeeze of the lever or press of the pedal. Let the rider behind you figure out what the hazard is. By the time you signal that it's there, you're already dealing with it and need all your wits about you.

The Leader

The ride leader should have experience both in riding and in leading group rides and should also have a superior riding strategy. The leader takes on a large

One important note about passing: Don't just pass a slow-moving vehicle and then park your bike 20 feet in front of it. Move over to the right side of the lane and keep your speed up so there's enough room for the riders behind you to pass, too. Don't leave a group of riders hanging out in the breeze.

Ignore Your Mirrors

Ever notice that road racers don't have mirrors on their bikes? It's too easy to stare too long into that window to the world behind you and miss your mark. Riding in your mirrors is a great way to completely overlook important information in your 11 to 1 zone. On a group ride, force yourself to

Group Riding Rule Number 7: One signal only: the brake light.

Pay special attention to your riding and dial it back a little bit after longer stops like lunch or an afternoon tea party. On hot or cold days, be aware of what fatigue, dehydration, and hypothermia can do to your skills over time.

The safest signal I can imagine is a brake light. It takes very little effort, you don't need to remove either hand from the bars, and it's unmistakable to those behind you. Red light equals something not ordinary equals slow down. Agree to it beforehand.

Group Riding Rule Number 8: If someone crashes, don't make it worse. Stay calm, find a safe place to park, and render aid as necessary.

amount of responsibility—leading the charge—but also the more subtle responsibility of keeping the group together, or at least not riding like such a wanker that the group has no chance of remaining a group. The ride leader should provide the map or route sheet, a basic verbal description of where the group is going, and information on any known hazard spots or tricky intersections. The leader should also try to set a pace comfortable for the slowest person in your group. Anyone who thinks the pace is too slow can ask to pass the leader.

Imagine you are the leader of a group of 10 or 20 riders. This would be at least 10 to 20 seconds long—that's 880 to 1,760 feet long at 60 miles per hour. Imagine you're pulling a trailer that is three to six football fields long, and ride accordingly. This, of course, would be impossible, but it should give you an idea of how you ideally need to ride in order to keep the group together and blend smoothly with other traffic. True, everyone is already riding his or her own ride, but it's still a nice touch to make transitions with the rest of the group in mind. Anticipate yellow lights and choose parking areas very carefully!

If you're a follower, make sure you inform the group if you have to split off

early. They'll probably be waiting for you at all the turns, remember? If you don't show, they may spend the rest of the day looking for you.

The Inevitable Crash

Crashes happen for all kinds of reasons—other motorists, sand or gravel in the road, spastic animals—but on group rides they seem to happen mostly because of riders' mental errors. Pay special attention to your riding and back off a little bit on your pace, especially after longer stops like lunch or afternoon tea. On hot or cold days, be aware of what fatigue, dehydration, and hypothermia can do to your skills over time. If you see another rider suddenly acting strangely on the

road, give them some more space, or if you're really worried for them, make a safe pass, look for a likely spot, then pull over smoothly to have a quick self-evaluation.

If a rider in your line of sight crashes, it is critical that you maintain your concentration and completely ignore the crash, then calmly and smoothly find a place to pull over and stop or turn around that won't endanger those behind you. No need to panic, that rider won't be going anywhere for a few minutes. They're not going to get any more injured or dead or crashed just because you didn't slam on your brakes and grind to a halt in the gravel shoulder. Don't exacerbate the situation by panicking.

Understand too that the rider behind you who just saw his or her first motorcycle crash is no longer at 100 percent attention. Make it easy for that person. Find a safe place to pull over, signal your intentions, flash your brake light, and make sure there's room for everyone to stop, just the way a ride leader would do. The key is to remain calm and forget about the crash until you have your bike parked safely off the roadway. Concentrate on the task at hand first. Don't make the crash worse by causing another.

A rider who crashes should generally quit the group ride and go home. (On a longer tour, of course, this is not so easy. Then it'd be best to hang it up for the day.) Putting your pride and joy into the weeds is troubling to most people, and for the rest of the day their head will probably not be in the game. That person needs to cool off, collect themselves, and then head for home on the easiest route possible. It is usually a good idea to send someone else along, just in case of mechanical trouble or latent injuries.

If your brain is up for the challenge, it's a nice gesture to offer to lead someone home. After a crash, a rider will be mentally replaying the events over and over and will likely forget about riding and forget about the road altogether. Offer to lead the rider home and give him or her specific instructions: "Follow me." It will then be your job to ride for both of you. It's not hard. In fact, it's very much like leading a group ride, except you know the person behind

Use extreme caution when riding under bridges in the rain. While the water washes away the grease, dirt, and crap that accumulates on the regular road surface, the bridge protects the road underneath it from this cleansing process. Even in dry weather, use caution under bridges because they rarely offer traction as good as the surrounding roads.

If your brain is up for the challenge, it's a nice gesture to offer to lead someone home after a crash. The rider will be mentally replaying the events over and over and will likely forget about riding and forget about the road altogether. Give them a safe target upon which to fixate.

Sightseeing on a bike is a compromise. If you're out to ride, then ride. Ignore the scenery. If you're out to enjoy the scenery, then stop frequently to do so. Reduce your speed if you decide to sightsee while riding.

you is at risk. Anticipate hazards better, signal earlier, brake sooner, turn smoother, and make frequent stops. Ride as if the rider behind you is drunk and can do nothing but follow your taillight. Give him or her a safe target upon which to fixate.

Riding in the Rain

Wet-weather riding is inevitable in the life of a dedicated motorcyclist and weighs in with a lot more risk than dry riding. A motorcyclist in the rain is very much like a fish in the rain (out of water, I mean.) You're still in your basic element, but you're not getting what you need from the environment. Your visibility is hampered, your traction is only a fraction of what it should be, and your attention is diverted slightly by the additional distractions these things incur. For every notch rainy travel bumps you down in the riding efficiency spectrum, you need to adjust your style to bring it back up. Use the gains from proper positioning, reduced speed and lean angles,

and increased attention to make up for added risk.

Visibility and Positioning

Your most important source of information has just been cut in half, as well as that of everyone else. It's far easier to find yourself in a place where another motorist can't see you, especially considering that the rain hampers their vision and attention, too. Some cleaning products are better than others when it comes to displacing water from your face shield in a storm—consider using car or furniture wax. Take steps to be extra visible with your positioning and clothing. Slow down to give yourself more time and space to react, and get off the main roads and onto the side roads where you have less chance of becoming lost in the wet, dark crowd.

Traction

Assume you have about half the traction that you do on a dry surface, and ride accordingly, but pay more attention to your surroundings and less to your tires. Take care to keep speeds and lean angles down, slow more and earlier for corners, slow more gradually for stops, and try not to let yourself become too distracted by the thought of sliding the tires. They'll stick. After all, they're riding on clean, wet pavement.

But remember, the same spots that are slippery when dry are like ice treated with bikini wax when wet. Sit out the first 20 minutes or so of any rainstorm to let the roads wash clean, and be particularly careful on the grease strip in the middle of the road, painted lines and markings, metal surfaces like railroad crossings and manhole covers, and especially under bridges—the rain doesn't wash the road under bridges as well, and it can stay slick for hours.

Attention

Drops of water on your visor, the hissing of the pavement beneath you, and the increase in humidity inside your helmet can all have a distracting effect. Add to these the restricted freedom of movement that rain gear forces upon you and you've got somewhere in the realm of only half as much mental acuity to devote to the environment. OK, so here we are: Vision is reduced by a goodly amount, traction is cut in half, and now your attention takes a hit as well? You've just taken a nosedive down the scale of motorcycle efficiency and need to do everything you can to maximize what efficiency you have remaining. Make it a point to reduce your rate of travel and concentrate harder on your surroundings than you normally do. If you have any chance of being distracted with thoughts or emotions while riding, get off the road, sort them out, and put them away before you get back on the bike. I'd estimate that riding in the rain, if you're not prepared for it both mentally and physically, is the equivalent of jumping up an entire risk level. You were at three before? Now you're at four. Take care.

Temperature Extremes

Heat and cold can severely affect your concentration, and you'll never know it until it's too late—this being the worst-case results of dehydration, heat stroke, or hypothermia. Know the weather forecast; prepare as well as you can with your riding gear, water intake, and diet; monitor yourself constantly; and plan your stops ahead of time, especially if you're on a long trip. Like drinking alcohol, your best bet is to decide how many drinks (miles) you will have or when you will quit (stop) *before* you start drinking (riding). Don't ignore the little warning signs that you've been on the road too long. Pull over and cool off or warm up until your mind is back where it should be. Stop to evaluate yourself at least twice as often as you normally would. Weather that is cold or hot enough to interfere with your physiological ability to think is the equivalent of jumping three risk levels. You were at three before? Consider yourself at six.

Drugs

Prescription and over-the-counter drugs can often have severe negative effects on attention, perception, and vision. When mixed with other medications, alcohol, herbal remedies, or certain foods, the effects can be unpredictable and downright dangerous when in the saddle. Additionally, it's difficult to estimate reactions from one person to the next. Everybody's different.

It is critical that you understand the side effects of any medications you're taking and that you avoid combining chemicals in your body. When in doubt, talk to your doctor. If a medication is known to have deleterious effects, it's smart to try the first few doses in a safe environment before venturing out into the world on your motorcycle.

Sightseeing

Soaking in the bursts of flowers and churned, fertilized earth in the springtime or the robust display of dying leaves in the fall are some of the best rewards of riding—the sights, the feel of the air, and the aromas all place you at the center of the universe when you're in the thick of it. But they're also a distraction, and the risk-averse rider needs to adapt his or her riding style. It's a compromise. If you're out to ride, then ride and ignore the scenery. If you're out to enjoy the scenery, then stop frequently to do so and reduce

When riding with a passenger, remember that you're riding for two. Technically, the risk doubles when that passenger gets on.

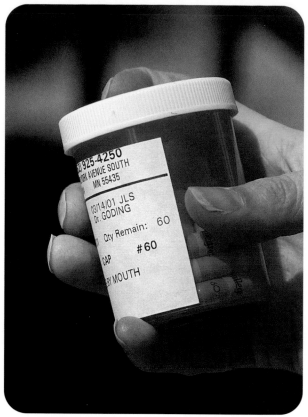

It is critical that you understand the side effects of any medications you're taking and that you avoid combining chemicals in your body.

your speed if you decide to sightsee while riding. Taking away even 10 percent of your concentration is not acceptable. If you risk that much concentration by bird watching, lower your speed enough to gain that much back.

Your Other Half

When riding two-up, your risk is directly related to the pillion's age, experience, and state of mind. Don't let your passenger send you both up the risk table. Until your passenger is an experienced and competent back-seater, reduce your risks by slowing down, being extra attentive, extra smooth, and leaving yourself more time and space to react. Remember, you're riding for two. Tech-

nically, the risk doubles when that passenger gets on.

Rider Fuel

Your choice of sustenance before and during a ride shouldn't just be a matter of what's available. Physiologically, some foods are better for riding than others.

Unfortunately, the right riding diet doesn't exist. Every rider is so different it would be impossible to outline the correct things to eat and drink when it comes to riding. Even dieticians have a hard time agreeing on simple nutritional theories. I encourage you to analyze what you eat, when you eat it, and how it makes you feel in order to best develop a routine when on the road. Do you function best on a full stomach or an empty one? Do you concentrate best after eating protein-rich foods (meat, eggs, dairy, nuts), carbohydrates (breads, noodles, fruits and vegetables), or fats (fast food, heavily salted gas-station snack treats)? Are you best after water, soda, coffee, or fruit juice? Hot food or cold food? The questions go on forever.

Before You Hit the Road

- Know where you are on the scale of 1 to 99.
- Avoid riding in groups.
- Don't allow rainy riding to distract you.
- Know the extreme effects of temperature.
- If you want to sightsee, drive a car.
- With a passenger, the risk doubles and then some.
- Know which foods afford you the best concentration.

INDEX

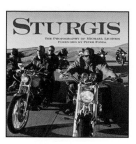
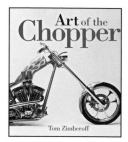
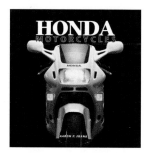

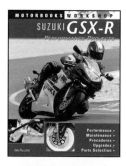
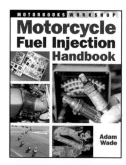